ARISTOCRACY

NEW PERSPECTIVES ON THE PAST

General Editor
R. I. Moore

Advisory Editors
Gerald Aylmer
Ioan Lewis
Patrick Wormald

Published

Ernest Gellner
NATIONS AND NATIONALISM

Jonathan Powis
ARISTOCRACY

In preparation

E. L. Peters
TORTURE IN THE WEST

Bernard Crick
REPRESENTATIVE INSTITUTIONS

R. M. Hartwell
CAPITALISM

R. I. Moore
PERSECUTION

David Gress
THE STATE

Eugene Kamenka
BUREAUCRACY

ARISTOCRACY

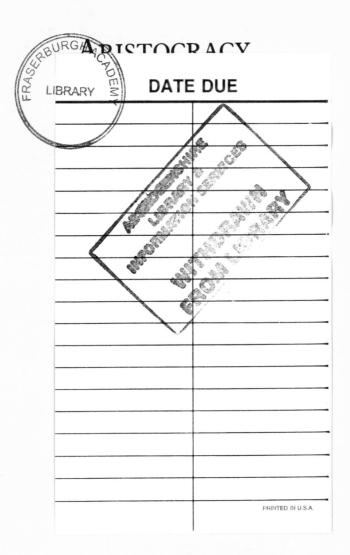

DATE DUE

PRINTED IN U.S.A.

First published 1984

Basil Blackwell Publisher Ltd
108 Cowley Road, Oxford OX4 1JF, UK

Basil Blackwell Inc.
432 Park Avenue South, Suite 1505,
New York, NY 10016, USA

British Library Cataloguing in Publication Data

Aristocracy.—(New perspectives on the past; 2)
1. Europe—Nobility—History
I. Title   II. Series
305.5'2'094   HT653.E9
ISBN 0–631–13067–5
0–631–13706–8 Pbk

Library of Congress Cataloging in Publication Data

Powis, Jonathan.
  Aristocracy.
  (New perspectives on the past)
  Bibliography: p. 103
  Includes index.
  1. Aristocracy–Europe.   2. Power (Social sciences)
I. Title.   II. Series.
HT653.E9P68 1984   305.5'2'094   84–12484

ISBN 0–631–13067–5
ISBN 0–631–13706–8 (Pbk.)

Typeset by Cambrian Typesetters, Frimley, Camberley, Surrey
Printed in Great Britain by Redwood Burn Ltd, Trowbridge,
Wilts.

Contents

Editor's Preface

Ignorance has many forms, and all of them are dangerous. In the nineteenth and twentieth centuries our chief effort has been to free ourselves from tradition and superstition in large questions, and from the error in small ones upon which they rest, by redefining the fields of knowledge and evolving in each the distinctive method appropriate for its cultivation. The achievement has been incalculable, but not without cost. As each new subject has developed a specialist vocabulary to permit rapid and precise reference to its own common and rapidly growing stock of ideas and discoveries, and come to require a greater depth of expertise from its specialists, scholars have been cut off by their own erudition not only from mankind at large, but from the findings of workers in other fields, and even in other parts of their own. Isolation diminishes not only the usefulness but the soundness of their labours when energies are exclusively devoted to eliminating the small blemishes so embarrassingly obvious to the fellow-professional in the next patch, instead of avoiding others that may loom much larger from, as it were, a more distant vantage point. Marc Bloch observed a contradiction in the attitudes of many historians: 'when it is a question of ascertaining whether or not some human act has really taken place, they cannot be too painstaking. If they proceed to the reasons for that act, they are content with the merest appearance, ordinarily founded upon one of those maxims of common-place psychology which are neither more nor less true than their opposites.' When the historian peeps across the fence he sees his neighbours, in literature, perhaps, or sociology, just as complacent in relying on historical platitudes which are naive, simplistic or obsolete.

New Perspectives on the Past is not a reaction against specialization, which would be a romantic absurdity, but an attempt to come to terms with it. The authors, of course, are specialists, and their thought and conclusions rest on the foundation of distinguished professional research in different periods and fields. Here they will free themselves, as far as it is possible, from the restraints of subject, region and period within which they ordinarily and necessarily work, to discuss problems simply as problems, and not as 'history' or 'politics' or 'economics'. They will write for specialists, because we are all specialists now, and for laymen, because we are all laymen.

The place of the aristocracy in European history can be understood only through such an approach as this. Its importance has seldom been doubted, and hardly more often examined. It has its part in every great historical movement, generally as a recalcitrant but foredoomed obstacle to the progressive forces upon which historians have fixed their attention — monarchies and their machinery of government, the commercial ethic, the professional middle classes with the triumph of whose values the rise of modern historical scholarship has itself been so intimately associated, and so on. But in this habitual characterization there is, as Jonathan Powis observes, a contradiction. A class so chronically outmoded has been an uncommonly long time adying, and its role in life has been more complicated and more creative than perpetual moribundity suggests. By considering aristocracy in a long chronological perspective, and in a comprehensive analytical framework, Powis offers a fresh understanding not only of the aristocrats themselves, with their distinctive patterns of thought and behaviour, the nature of their power and their relations with the state, but of the thousand years of European development during which they were at the centre of the stage.

R. I. Moore

Foreword

The immediate origin of this book was in an invitation to contribute a volume to the series of which it forms a part. Its roots, however, go deeper: to a number of years' experience in teaching a course on 'Aristocracies' at the University of York, and (earlier still) to the attempts of a novice graduate student to carry out some fairly detailed investigations into the privileged classes of sixteenth-century France. The focus of the book, like the background of its author, is Western European. Its material is drawn from the history of those communities whose peoples spoke, and speak, Germanic or Romance vernaculars: languages which the author can read for himself and in which he feels to varying degrees at home. This is a statement of the author's limitations; it implies no view about whether the phenomena which the book seeks to describe are specifically Western European ones. That judgement may best be left to others, especially perhaps to those whose interests lie in the world beyond Europe.

To attempt an interpretative essay of this kind is to accumulate innumerable debts for assistance rendered along the way. Short of embarking on a full-scale academic autobiography, I must acknowledge three obligations above all: to the Department of History at the University of York, to Bob Moore, most vigilant and constructive of editors, and to my wife.

J.K.P.

Introduction

History, remarked the political scientist Pareto, is a graveyard of aristocracies. Hereditary ruling groups – a working definition of what an aristocracy is – have had a hand in shaping much of the European past. A book on the subject might usefully follow Pareto's cue, and compare the fortunes of different aristocracies *en route* to the inevitable graveyard: their rise and decline, their exercise and eventual loss of power. But a strictly comparative approach raises serious problems. The nature of the evidence may hamper effective comparison. On the important issue of recruitment, for example – of how newcomers entered the charmed circle – the recent past has left an immense quantity of documentation; but for medieval or Renaissance times the historian has to confront material – genealogies or letters of ennoblement – which is scrappy when not deliberately misleading. The loss of aristocratic power – the circumstances in which different aristocracies had their hold over the community broken – is certainly an issue well suited to comparative treatment, and there will be something to say about it in the final chapter. But, in the main, the argument which follows is organized along rather different lines.

Some implications of Pareto's remark are in any case misleading. Different aristocracies have indeed come and gone: instances of those ever-circulating elites which so fascinated the Italian writer. But, for all their differences, aristocracies in the West have shared certain common features. In Pareto's terms they were elites of a highly distinctive kind. And the features which made them distinctive have shown a striking capacity for adaptation and survival over the years. The 'feudal states' of the eleventh and twelfth centuries, the bustling commercial environment of Renaissance Venice, the already industrial landscape of early Victorian England – the historical settings could scarcely have differed more. But, in all three, the force of aristocracy was inescapable: power lay with families of high social rank; rank was bequeathed by birth, or imparted by education and social osmosis; and the association between rank and power received general (if not unquestioned) acceptance in the community at large. In this perspective, the rise and fall of different aristocracies begin to appear less significant than the tenacity of the aristocratic link between power and rank: the assumption that throughout the life of a community, leadership properly lies with those who enjoy an innate, special claim to it. By Victorian times that assumption was, of course, under challenge, and in the end (to echo Pareto) it indeed arrived at the graveyard. But it took a very long time to get there. And the present book will focus on this perhaps most fundamental sense of the term: aristocracy as a distinctive kind of power exercised by a distinctive group of people.

Whatever the precise meaning they attach to the word, historians have often found aristocracy both an elusive and an unsympathetic subject. This may reflect a proper distaste for the presence of vast accumulations of hereditary wealth in communities beset by chronic poverty. Practical difficulties may also be relevant. The systematic study of aristocratic power depends heavily on the accessibility of family papers. Over much of Western Europe such material has only slowly (and often very recently) been transferred into the public archives or otherwise made available to scholars. And a great deal still remains inaccessible in private hands. But perhaps the most important factor of all has been the nature of history's development as an organised field of study. During the later nineteenth and early twentieth centuries, research was directed above all to the history of institutions: to the growth of Parliament and the royal administration in England, and to the emerging national states of France, Germany and Italy on the Continent. Amid such concerns aristocratic power appeared a marginal force, even a reactionary or disruptive one. Noblemen had made occasional contributions to the cause of progress, it was true, from the barons at Runnymede to Count Cavour's part in the unification of Italy. But the consensus was less favourable. In a historical perspective dominated by the growth of public institutions and the rise of an enlightened middle class, aristocratic power was easily associated with decadence and feudal anarchy.

Over recent decades, a rather different picture has begun to emerge. This is not to say that historians have been seduced into a new fondness for birth and privilege. (A survey of the expanding seigneurial jurisdictions of early medieval Provence recently summed up the process as 'a legitimizing mask for class terror' against the peasantry.) But class terror or not, a wider range of documentation has made possible far fuller examination of the actual character of aristocracy. Rapid growth in the study of social history has made the sheer fact of aristocratic power (and its tenacity down the centuries) increasingly visible. That tenacious hold requires analysis: and so far as possible analysis which discards anachronistic assumptions about the inevitability of decline.

The chapters which follow move from status to wealth, and then to power, and the part which each played in the history of aristocracy. Throughout much of the Western past, aristocratic status has been defined in terms of nobility, of inclusion in a distinct social group. The words are not strictly synonyms. However we define it, 'aristocracy' carries associations of authority and leadership; 'nobility' does not. (Families of impeccable noble rank frequently found themselves impoverished and wholly without influence in public life.) But common usage has tended to be less precise. Indexes and catalogues often treat the terms as interchangeable: '*for Aristocracy see under* Nobility' (or vice versa). Aristocracy after all had its roots in a world of more or less formal noble privilege. Authority was largely in the hands of families and individuals whose title to leadership included their distinctive noble rank.

Two preoccupations were of particular importance in shaping aristocratic assumptions about rank: these were honour and heredity. Anthropologists tell us that in communities with few or no formal institutions, the maintenance of honour provides a means for controlling individual behaviour. There is no necessary connection between the honour code and the existence of a clear-cut social hierarchy. But for much of the Western past, honour and rank have been closely related, and rank was hereditary. Some individuals (or, better, families) inherited and transmitted a greater stock of honour than the majority of their contemporaries. Where wide disparities of wealth and power existed, and where movement between classes was limited, the mystique surrounding

birth was no mere irrationality. 'Ancestry' provided a convenient
shorthand for all the advantages of privileged upbringing and
connection. Honour itself became an ancestral possession. But
the idea of honour, like that of privilege, exercised its force far
beyond a narrowly aristocratic milieu. It was a currency in which
people of modest rank could deal, even if their stock of it were
small; and the aristocratic hold over the rest of the community
may have been all the greater as a result. Nor should we think of
nobilities as too literally 'exclusive'. All noble families were in
principle long established, but they had all had to start
somewhere. Without courting extinction, no aristocracy could
permanently say 'Keep out'. So at varying speeds in different
contexts newcomers were recruited, both to the enjoyment of
privilege and to the exercise of leadership; and new dynasties
grew up.

The preoccupation with family, rank and honour shaped the
uses of aristocratic wealth. There are, of course, some inescapable
links between the control of material resources and the survival of
aristocracy over the centuries. Wealth was vital, both for individual families and for the maintenance of public leadership in noble
hands. Whether in the agrarian economy of the earlier Middle
Ages or in the booming commercial activity of Genoa and Venice
during the fifteenth and sixteenth centuries, the richest families
in the community were of noble rank. Aristocracy did not in the
long run retain its hold once the lion's share of wealth passed into
the control of financiers and industrialists. But these generalizations tell only a part of the story. It was what nobles did with their
wealth that mattered: they were different, but not just because
they were richer than other people. Some forms of economic
activity were closed to them, some kinds of property theirs alone
to purchase or inherit. Indeed dynastic interests often ensured
that an individual's control over his 'property' was itself severaly
limited. Noblemen had to strike a balance between the future
needs of their house and the current obligation to live – which
meant to *spend* – in accordance with their rank. Historians have
not always been sensitive to the logic of large-scale aristocratic
expenditure. If lavish display was so constantly indulged in, it
was in large part a matter of meeting the community's expectations of how great families should live. This may offend modern
advocates of prudent housekeeping, but the visible extravagance

of aristocratic wealth was not, in its context, irrational or empty of meaning.

The needs of the house — dead ancestors and subsequent generations included — shaped the uses to which wealth was put. And the family was at the heart of aristocratic power. Ties of kinship ranged outward from the household into a wider circle of friends and dependants. For better or worse, a great man's network of relatives and followers gave him, and them, a public role. 'Clientage' and 'connection' are not necessarily terms of approval. Historians of government or of the law have often seen these patterns of aristocratic association as an archaic or disruptive force. But formal governing institutions are not the sole means by which disputes can be resolved and violence limited. A nobleman's authority over members of his entourage might enable him to act as arbiter or protector within the community at large.

As the public authority of the state grew, these forms of aristocratic leadership appeared increasingly anomalous. An abundant literature suggests the possibility of conflict between the claims of lord over followers on the one hand and of state over subjects on the other. In the short run contretemps certainly occurred, and in the far longer run the distinctive claims of aristocratic authority finally yielded. But over centuries of gradual adaptation, governments (largely in any case staffed by noblemen) tended to compromise: the local influence of aristocratic patrons might be harnessed, and prestigious recruits drawn into state service. In expanding government machines, aristocratic connection survived and prospered. It was certainly possible for new men to rise through the administrative ranks, but by the time they reached the top the material and psychological attractions of nobility were likely to have left their mark. Giving orders long remained a gentleman's business, after all, and newcomers who gave orders quickly acquired the trappings of a gentleman.

These, crudely sketched, are some of the principal features of aristocracy as it operated down to the recent past. To construct a timeless ideal type would be absurd. One of the strengths of aristocracy has been a slow adjustment to material and cultural change. But the relation between birth, rank and power proved strikingly tenacious. And the potency of that link down the centuries is a theme worth emphasizing in a subject too easily treated in terms of crisis and decline.

1

Status and Hierarchy

'Aristocracy' made its first appearance among the Greeks. for them, the term meant rule by the best. Aristotle approved of aristocracy, and insisted on the contrast between it and its corrupt variant, oligarchy. He was more realistic than some of his predecessors, and defined aristocracy as rule by the few rather than by the best; but he thought it no less worth recommending on that account. Whether power lay with the few or with the best, and whatever the relation between these categories might be, classical notions of aristocracy centred on the power of some men to command the rest. So it remained down to the Renaissance and beyond. When Montesquieu published *The Spirit of the Laws* in 1748, his use of 'aristocracy' echoed that of the ancient world: a republic where high-minded magistrates wielded authority over the citizenry to the greater good of the community as a whole. *Authority* is crucial. As we shall see, aristocracy has become a term open to uses very different from those of classical antiquity. But from ancient times until the very recent past — so this book will argue — aristocracy has always implied the right, and duty, of one group of people to give orders to the rest of their contemporaries.

Problems of definition nevertheless arise. Today, 'aristocracy' denotes not things but men and women. Already in the eighteenth century, writers were using the term to describe the people who ran the system of government as much as the system itself. By the time of the French Revolution, it was becoming possible to apply 'aristocracy' to a whole social class, and to coin a new (and hostile) word for those found within it: 'aristocrat'. In the rank-conscious Europe of the Old Regime it was hardly surprising if 'rule by the best' meant that in practice the power of command was vested in those of high social standing. A revolution which took as its aim the overthrow of that political system naturally enough lumped together the system and the class which appeared to be its chief beneficiary. 'Aristocracy' was beginning to imply a description of social relations, of certain people and their activities. And in the context of the later eighteenth century, description often gave place to violent polemic for and against the rights of 'aristocracy', with aristocracy now conceived as a privileged ruling order.

So the sense of the word was shifting, but there was nothing new about the word itself. Nor was there much new about the social group to which it was coming to refer. The languages of western Europe abound in the terminology of privilege and distinction, variously applicable to different sorts and conditions of people at different times and in different places: 'nobility', *nobleza*, *Adel* and a myriad more. What privilege amounted to in practice was similarly various. Formal recognition of noble rights by monarchical governments took concrete form in the widespread exemption of nobles from payment of direct taxes. Informal customary acceptance of social distinction may have been no less important. Some historians have doubted, for example, whether an English nobility can properly be said ever to have existed, since the upper classes on the northern side of the Channel never enjoyed the fiscal privileges of their continental counterparts. But in Tudor times writers regularly described an English *nobilitas* made up of greater and lesser *nobiles*, peers and untitled gentlemen respectively. This was no mere theorizing. It was from men of proper and distinctive rank – peers and gentlemen – that appointments were made to the crucial local offices or Lord-Lieutenants and Justices of the Peace. In the colleges of early modern Oxford and Cambridge, young men of good family, with the misleading name of 'fellow-commoners', enjoyed distinctive dining rights and academic privileges. The distinctiveness of the well-born was visible everywhere, whether or not underwritten by government decree. Aristocracy as we now understand it implies both the existence of that distinctiveness, and its translation into the visible trappings of distinction: from tax-exemption to the wearing of appropriate, and different, clothes.

For reasons already touched on, it seems only to have been in the eighteenth century that 'aristocracy' came to be applied to this privileged world and its inhabitants. In earlier periods, the term retained its classical — that is its specifically political — connotations. And when in earlier periods men discussed those who enjoyed conspicuous rank or status, they called them not aristocrats but gentlemen or nobles. These shifting usages cause problems, but they are hardly insuperable. It is a commonplace historical observation that at different periods different words have been used to describe similar things and that different things have been called by the same name. 'Aristocracy' in modern usage has a content largely distinct from Aristotle's use of the word, and far closer to such medieval notions as *noblesse* or the community of the well-born. We need not press these terms too close to the definition of aristocracy suggested in the introduction. Honourable birth and status provided no guarantee against genteel poverty, or against deficiency in what contemporaries took to be talent: they were not in themselves a passport to leadership and renown. So 'aristocracy' was not merely another, relatively late synonym for the noble and the well-born. Not all those who enjoyed privileged noble status could hope to reach for the commanding authority which aristocracy seems inescapably to imply.

Nevertheless, power and privilege have remained intimately connected over the centuries. For the ancients, aristocracy was a purely political term: the leadership of some men over others. But until a very recent stage of Western history, leadership has itself been coloured by considerations of social rank. Rank has been a necessary — if not a sufficient — qualification for aspiring leaders, and successful leaders have been rewarded by enhanced rank. Arthur Wellesley was born the third son of an earl, and died Duke of Wellington. Later chapters will suggest some of the ways in which distinctive aristocratic rank shaped the character of aristocratic power over others. Here something more needs to be said about what made that rank distinctive, and in particular about the two preoccupations which bulked so large in thinking about noble status: honour and family.

Honour and rank

The preoccupation with honour was constant, but its meaning shifted a good deal over time; and even in a historical context honour could manifest itself in a number of different ways. 'Death rather than dishonour' — a commonplace of aristocratic morality down the centuries — implies that honour was a matter of proper conduct. A code existed; dishonour was the penalty for its violation. This was clearly an element in the system. In 1536 the north of England, or part of it, rose in revolt against political and religious changes imposed by the government of Henry VIII. Lord Darcy held Pontefract Castle for the rebels, and royal officers called on him to surrender. He refused, saying 'What is a man but his promise?' Darcy's promise had been to the rebels, and to break it would have been to act dishonourably. More than behaviour was probably at stake here. Honour also meant esteem or reputation, and Darcy was no doubt quite aware of the point. Good name was a property, an asset; a man might squander it by his own misconduct, or (as Iago told Othello) others might 'filch' it from him. The code of honour regulated individual behaviour, but its logic left little room for such abstractions as the appeal to the individual's conscience. The community expected the man of honour to act honourably; and to the extent that he did so it considered his honour, or reputation, intact. The precise character of honourable conduct varied greatly over the centuries, and there will be a good deal to say about these variations in due course. The point here is the operation of the system, and its channelling of behaviour in directions which contemporary opinion deemed honourable. As Montesquieu said, men of honour are subject to the censure even of those who have none. When the commissioners on the reform of the civil service were collecting evidence in 1853, one witness insisted that future recruits must display a sense of honour, which he elaborated as including a healthy regard for public opinion, and 'the desire of being well thought of by a circle of friends'. Esteem continued to matter.

Honour meant proper conduct, reflected in a reputation defended or enhanced. And it sometimes acquired yet another sense: the material benefits which closed the cycle, rewarding honourable conduct and a good name. In contemporary Britain, 'honours lists' continue to embody this particular usage. (And periodic rows over those admitted to the lists may suggest the lingering potency of the idea of honour, as well as a late twentieth-century uncertainty over just what the idea involves.) But the usage was far older, if not always less contentious. The great estates and titles which the Conqueror assigned to his victorious associates after 1066 − to Hugh 'of Chester' and Alan 'of Richmond' and men like them − were styled 'honours'. It was honours in the form of titles and privileges that the financially hard-pressed monarchs of the sixteenth and seventeenth centuries sold off in profusion. And the honours which rewarded distinction took a variety of more everyday forms: honourable places at table, honourable seats in church, honourable positions in public processions − and, for those who fell foul of the law, honourable methods of execution, usually by the sword. (In 1760 Lord Ferrers was hanged at Tyburn for the murder of his steward. The case attracted great attention, and appeared to some contemporaries a demonstration of the egalitarian character of English justice: peer or commoner, wrongdoers met their end on the gallows. But the episode made its impact precisely because a quite different assumption was so widely current. Did the honour of an earl − even a murderer − not entitle him to a more dignified departure from the scene?)

The notion of honour thus covered a number of processes. Honour, and the fear of incurring shame, might encourage individuals towards acceptable conduct, the maintenance of reputation, and the possibility of material or symbolic benefit. Where governing institutions are weak or absent, so anthropologists have suggested, concern for honour and fear of shame may indeed help to control individual behaviour. But are all individuals in such communities regarded as equally capable of striving for the honourable and avoiding the shameful? In some contexts this may be so; but in his essay on 'Honour' in the *International Encyclopaedia of the Social Sciences* Professor Pitt-Rivers has pointed out that where a clearly defined social hierarchy exists, an individual's birth is likely to be decisive in shaping assumptions about his capacity for honourable action. Today's honours lists may suggest, accurately or otherwise, a kind of free market in honours where meritorious individuals compete for their prizes. We can speculate that for much of the European past, assumptions would have been very different.

Indeed many of the views which have been heard in the preceding paragraphs make very clear just what assumptions underlay them. Montesquieu's man of honour knew that his reputation was exposed to the gaze of people whose status was utterly, and permanently, different from his own. Romilly's evidence before the civil service reform commissioners had stressed the need for future candidates to be sensitive to the dictates of honour and reputation: and such qualities, he thought, were unlikely to be found among the lower orders. The honour code, in all its ramifications, easily came to be seen as a code for those of rank. 'Honorifics' such as precedence on public occasions – or access to the more dignified forms of capital punishment – came in effect to mark out the distinctiveness of good family.

So the principles of the honour code were put into practice in communities which were themselves in varying degrees hierarchical. The mechanics of the code – maintaining one's reputation, arming oneself with visible signs of honour – were to a greater or lesser extent coloured by considerations of birth and status. Lowly origins might condemn some men (perhaps a majority) to the permanent disdain of their more honourable superiors. One English observer of the later sixteenth century contrasted the heirs of Adam, who inherited high rank, with those of Cain, who were (a daunting phrase) 'destinated to dishonour'. But this sounds extreme: more like religious moralism than any kind of social description. At no stage of its documented history was the social structure of the West likely to furnish a clear-cut division between those who participate in the honour code and those who do not. Modest assertions of honour and 'good name' could be found among groups of people with no claim to formal nobility. When the jurist Loyseau surveyed the French population shortly after 1600, he thought it quite proper for merchants or notaries to employ such titles as 'Maître' or 'Honorable Homme'. These were men with a proper, if limited, call on the esteem of others. Only further down the scale were groups to be found with no title to honour of any kind; this was the 'vile and mechanical' world of manual labour. A work such as Calderon's *Alcalde de Zalamea*, from rather later in the seventeenth century, draws its force from the same point. The small-town mayor of the title lacks the noble rank of the military commander who rapes his daughter; but he has a family name to defend, and he defends it to the death. In 1791 F. W. von Ramdohr, a Hanoverian civil servant, observed that one of the strengths of the European monarchies lay in the existence of professions and corporations with their own sense of collective honour – *Standesehre:* men such as the clergy, or university professors. This may be of some importance. Notions of honour, like a preoccupation with legal privileges, percolated far down the social order – certainly far beyond the lowest reaches of the nobility. The reputation and the marks of precedence appropriate to a *bourgeois* of Paris were small things compared to those of a prince of the blood. Derision or hostility greeted those who claimed a consideration above that due to their rank. But when the prince spoke of 'honour', in all its senses, he was appealing to a set of values of which the *bourgeois* – in infinitely less spectacular form – had some practical experience. The aristocratic hold on the rest of the community involved more than main force.

Within the ranks of the nobility itself, claims were sometimes made that all gentlemen were essentially equal, and thus equal in their claims to honour. Such a view was no doubt encouraged by the assorted rights and privileges which in various contexts the nobility shared, and which marked them out from their social inferiors. Nobles were not the only people to enjoy privileges of one kind or another, but certain privileges – tax-exemptions, distinctive inheritance-laws, a monopoly on certain public offices – were at different times and in different places associated with noble status. This may have bred a degree of solidarity. When Lord Palmerston attacked proposals for alterations to the laws of intestacy in 1859, he claimed to be acting in defence of the aristocracy as a whole, which he took to mean all landed gentlemen, titled or otherwise. A pamphlet which appeared in Paris in 1715 proclaimed that gentlemen must recognize their essential common interest: 'and that the honour of every noble is as good as that of every other.' But the strident tone tells its own story. Many thought otherwise, that particular sections of the nobility had a claim to honours of a distinctive and exceptional sort. (In early eighteenth-century France it was the dukes who were staking out claims of this kind.) As Hobbes pointed out, men continually compete for 'honour and dignity'. Consciousness of the interests of the nobility in relation to non-nobles was perfectly compatible with an intense rivalry between nobles for rank and precedence.

A pecking-order of rank (and honour) can be glimpsed in many Western nobilities far back in the Middle Ages. According to the customs of twelfth-century Catalonia, a viscount could claim 120

ounces of gold as compensation in a case of serious wounding; the
rate for a *caballer* (knight) was six ounces — and for a peasant,
two. The later middle ages saw a general elaboration of ranks and
titles of honour. England had traditionally known only one mark
or particular distinction within the nobility — that of earl — but
the first ducal title appeared in 1337. This was probably
conceived as a style restricted to members of the royal house, but
the restriction soon lapsed, and in the following century a number
of other new titles made their appearance: marquis, baron by writ
or patent, viscount. For men such as the Neville earls of
Westmorland, or the Montagu earls of Salisbury, the chances of
politics and war — civil as well as foreign — brought accession to
conspicuous honours. Something of the same kind happened in
fourteenth-century Castile, where the triumph of the royal house
of Trastámara swept relatively modest supporters like the
Mendoza family to the illustrious rank of grandee.

'*Relatively* modest' is an important qualification. These were
families of established local standing in the North riding or in Old
Castile. Turbulent times provided them with an opportunity to
acquire honour, and to display it, with unprecedented *eclat*. They
were rising in the ranks of the privileged. War would long
continue to offer chances for men of distinction to add their own
quota to the stock which they had inherited, as the case of
Wellesley/Wellington reminds us. There might be other avenues
of opportunity, perhaps increasingly numerous with the passage
of time. A sound education, and a talent for public affairs, took
the son of a substantial Northamptonshire gentleman into the
inner counsels of Queen Elizabeth. The Cecil family was not
without standing or honour when William was born in 1520; but
the great houses at Burghley and Hatfield are a visible demonstration of the spectacular further advances that lay in store.
Government service, like success on the battlefield, offered a
means of moving from solid local respectability to national pre-
eminence.

So within the ranks of the nobility, marks of distinction
proliferated. Men of ability and ruthlessness clambered from one
rank of honour to another, and took note of the changing styles
and fashions they encountered along the way. Conduct and
presentation underscored more formal gradations within honourable society — or 'Society'. The extremely grand Lord Chester-

field, writing in the middle of the eighteenth century, was appalled to find spurs and deerskin waistcoats worn in the Pump Room at Bath. This was the dress of booby squires who might, at a pinch, rate as gentlemen. Top people — like Chesterfield — had other standards. But who were top? Certainly, as we have seen, determined and (variously) talented individuals might hope to rise from mere gentility to more or less conspicuous titles of honour. Those who did so passed on the fruits of their achievement to their heirs, if any. The fourth Earl of Chesterfield, after all, was the eldest son of the third earl. Again, and more explicitly, the question arises of the relation between honour and birth. In communities in which social mobility was likely to be more or less limited, most of those who enjoyed high rank, as well as such more elusive qualities as prestige or 'style', were in a position to do so because they were the successors of their parents. This was true at all levels, from the dazzling heights of the aristocracy, through the honourable gentility of knights and lesser landowners, to the marks of respect due to such non-noble worthies as lawyers or merchants. Rank and honour formed a hierarchy, an order that was until very recent times taken to be natural.

A few individuals might enjoy meteoric upward progress. But the metaphor is significant. Human society was long held to embody a principle of hierarchy which governed the creation as a whole. When Renaissance writers pondered the careers of great men risen from obscurity, they compared them to shooting stars: running counter to a universal hierarchy in which the creator allotted each man — like each planet — his natural place. And a man's natural place was overwhelmingly determined by his birth; 'birth' is, after all, what the Latin word *natura* frequently means. The link between rank and ancestry has for much of the European past itself been regarded as natural. As late as the mid-nineteenth century, the Reverend William Sewell liked to remind the boys of Radley College that they must honour the baby in the cradle for the sake of its (aristocratic) father.

Family

Hence the noble preoccupation with family: as great as — indeed scarcely distinguished from – their obsession with honour. Throughout Western Europe increasing literacy among lay people from the later Middle Ages onward produced a barrage of more or less reliable family memoirs. John Smyth's *Lives of the Berkeleys* appeared in 1618 and was better documented than many, but his claim to be the first genealogical historian of any 'patrimonial' family is probably excessive. Visible evidence of the preoccupation with descent survives in the library at Langley Marish, Buckinghamshire, where Sir John Kederminster's family tree, painted over the fireplace, dominates the room. Attention to genealogy may have been increased by the activities of governments. Such agencies as the English College of Arms sought to regulate and document claims to hereditary nobility. On the Continent, noble exemption from direct taxation gave the authorities a particular interest in the matter. By the end of the fifteenth century the Spanish crown had established 'judges of nobility' at Valladolid and Granada for the scrutiny of claims to noble – and tax-exempt – status; proof of honourable descent over a number of generations (usually three) was an important point in the claimant's favour.

Investigations of titles to nobility were to become a regular feature of life in early modern Europe, and this external scrutiny may have heightened interest in genealogy. But the association between honour, rank and descent ran far deeper than that. The modern use of 'aristocracy' carries associations with heredity quite lacking in its classical Greek usage. In Britain during the 1960s some significance was read into the descent of the then Prime Minister, the fourteenth Earl of Home; long ancestry might appear an important component of inherited – and in that context, by implication, undesirable – privilege. Public opinion was not greatly impressed, and seemed in the main to accept the retort that the leader of the Opposition was himself the fourteenth Mr Wilson. There was, so to speak, nothing special about aristocratic descent. If this was indeed the general view, then it marks a recent and decisive break with traditional assumptions. For centuries, it was precisely 'ancient lineage' which had made nobles special and contributed to the distinctive character of the honours they claimed.

For the remoter past, the topic becomes more elusive. Evidence thins out, both of attitudes towards the family, and for the construction of reliable genealogies. Hence uncertainties among historians about the position of nobles in the earlier Middle Ages, and in particular the ninth and tenth centuries. Marc Bloch argued that in this period of chronic disorder – Carolingian government in decay, the West under assault from Islam and the Vikings – all sense of a hereditary nobility was lost. Yet recent work suggests that this may not be the whole story. In old Roman centres, such as Trier or Limoges, leading families often maintained connections with particular shrines or tombs. Actual descent from Roman times was frequently impossible to establish, but the attempt to trace, or to fabricate, an ancestry – what German historians call *Ansippung* – may have its own significance. There are some signs, too, that a number of powerful dynasties survived from Carolingian times to wield authority as castellans and feudal overlords from the eleventh century onward. The evolving vocabulary of feudalism itself took on a hereditary note. In 1037 a celebrated constitution of the Emperor Conrad II proclaimed that land held as fief should pass unimpeded through the male heirs of that vassal. *Miles* – knight – in principle designated a function, that of service in war, rewarded by more or less conditional title to land; but here too blood came to count, and the sons of knights frequently styled themselves *milites* without taking on defined military duties. And in the early thirteenth century the Emperor Frederick II ruled that, without imperial mandate, no one was to claim the rank of knight – *honorem militum* – who was not himself of knightly stock – *de genere militum*. Once again, distinctive rank implied distinctive descent.

   In the middle ages and after, one group found itself particularly concerned with the hereditary preoccupations of nobles. What place were *churchmen* to allow the claims of blood? The maintenance of one's reputation, the assertion of pride in one's descent, were not after all among the more obvious preoccupations of the founder of Christianity. But the church had to work in the world, and to come to terms with the fact of noble power. This might mean attempting to limit aristocratic violence, or turning it to acceptable use. By the early twelfth century preachers such as Bernard of Clairvaux were asserting the positive christian merit earned by knights warring against the infidel. These principles took physical form in the new military-religious orders — the Knights of St John and of the Temple — and no doubt contributed something to the prestigious 'military honour' mentioned earlier.

Confrontation between church and nobility was in any case unthinkable. Clergy, both regular and secular, needed the physical protection — sometimes no doubt from other nobles — which fighting men could supply; they needed their financial contributions; and it was from among the nobility that they largely recruited to their own ranks. The tradition that high birth was a potent qualification for high ecclesiastical office can be glimpsed early. Already in Carolingian times chroniclers grumbled when low-born candidates obtained archbishoprics or abbacies. The Emperor can grant privileges, such as freeing slaves, wrote one observer early in the ninth century, but to make nobles is beyond his power 'because it's impossible'. Top jobs demanded noble rank, and nobility was a matter of time and ancestry, not government decree. Spokesmen for the hereditary nobility were to make these points over the centuries down almost to the present, but medieval churchmen provide some particularly vigorous expositions of the case. Of course, religious considerations might suggest a counter-argument. The vices of the nobility — pride, cruelty, worldly ambition — might be attacked: the equality of all in Christ proclaimed. The counter-argument existed, and — as we shall see — it was on occasion to entail drastic practical consequences for the nobility.

But for much of the time these radical implications were ignored or muffled. The biographer of Abbot Maieul described his subject's withdrawal from worldly things to the monastery of Cluny, late in the tenth century; but he found it impossible to omit a courteous account of the abbot's distinguished ancestry along the way. Open attacks on noble vice may themselves imply a high view of aristocratic religious responsibility. Of those to whom birth had given much, much might reasonably be demanded. The nobly born Aquinas thought a concern with honour the most potent inducement towards good conduct, and what better conduct than the energetic patronage of the church? So those of honourable descent might carry special and distinctive responsibility in matters of religion. Assumptions of this kind long outlived the Middle Ages. In 1640 the clergy of San Paolo Maggiore, Naples, petitioned their patron, the Prince of Sant'

Agata, for the construction of a new chapel on the grandest
possible plan; they hoped – in a significant phrase – 'that it
would stand as an example to all the other princes of the city'.
When the Duke of Montausier was buried at Paris in 1690, the
preacher warned those present to beware dynastic pride, and
went on to describe the 'seven centuries of glittering examples' in
the Duke's ancestry. And throughout the sixteenth and seventeenth centuries, the Protestant doctrine of 'the godly magistrate'
drew some of its strength from this source. Men born to authority
– the Lords of the Congregation in mid-sixteenth century
Scotland, the Elizabethan gentleman-sponsors of Puritan preach-
ing – inherited special religious duties as well.

The force of heredity was thus, apparently, inescapable.
Religious language frequently seemed to reinforce more secular
discussions of rank and honour: to drive home an imagined
hierarchy in which men's place was determined by birth (or
nature). Some social theorists struck an openly racialist note.
At the height of the religious and social troubles which swept later
sixteenth-century France, the royal magistrate Michel Hurault
wrote, in 1591, that the nobility enjoyed 'an innate superiority, a
born right to mastery' over the rest of the population. Medical
opinion pondered the mysterious virtues of blood and semen,
which transmitted honour from the father's generation to that of
the son. In the treatise on education which he published in 1533,
Cardinal Sadoleto reminded kings to devote as much attention to
aristocratic stock-breeding – he encouraged marriage between
the most illustrious houses – as they would to that of their horses
or their hunting-dogs. And kings were themselves the most
striking embodiment of the potency of blood and ancestry.

Such arguments were the common stock of writing on the
nobility in what might loosely be called pre-Enlightenment
Europe. Distinctions of honour and status ranged from the
glittering to the modest. In the individual's hopes of achieving a
greater or lesser stock of distinction, birth was crucial. (In
communities with little social mobility, a general admission of the
advantages of birth might serve to defuse the grievances of the
less advantaged.) Yet the association between blood, rank and
leadership posed its own problems. High birth might predispose
men to high authority, but it was no necessary protection against
the hazards of everyday life. Of the sixteen magnate families

which dominated the diocese of Osnabrück during the twelfth century, ten had died out by the end of the thirteenth. This was probably typical enough. The extinction of noble lineages has often been popularly associated with aristocratic violence; the English baronage allegedly committed collective suicide on the battlefields of the Wars of the Roses. Reality was more humdrum. Noble families, like others, intermittently fell victim to disease and infertility. Later fourteenth-century Castile experienced acute and violent instability during and after the reign of Pedro the Cruel; but of the twenty-six grandee families which disappeared during the period, half failed for the prosaic reason that they ran out of male heirs. A desire to avoid fragmenting the estate may have encouraged some families to limit the number of marriages in each generation, and this was a calculation which could easily go wrong. The slow numerical dwindling of the Venetian nobility during the seventeenth and eighteenth centuries is in part to be associated with the choice of large numbers of gentlemen to remain bachelors, with or without pressure from their families to do so.

For whatever reason, dynasties of the nobly-born failed to achieve collective immortality. Nobilities needed constant replenishment. Public authorities, too, might from time to time see fit to increase the numbers of the conspicuously honourable. The numerous new titles created by the English government after 1603 are a case in point. The scale of honours promised the new Stuart regime cash benefits and increased political support. And for the new knights or baronets there was the prospect of a conspicuous rise from the station to which they had been born. For all the mysteries of blood and lineage, movement into, and within, the hierarchy of honour was both possible and necessary. As Lord Lovat told the House of Lords in 1957, aristocracy, like a grouse-moor, requires regular restocking.

Newcomers

But within the framework of traditional ideas of rank and status, how was such recruitment to be justified? A good deal seems to turn on the career and background of the potential candidate for title or privilege. Military distinction has traditionally been taken as an indicator of honourable potential in those of modest birth. Tacitus noted that the tribes of barbarian Germany chose their kings according to ancestry, but their military commanders on merit (*virtus*). Many of the 'knights' who feature so energetically in the history of Europe after 1000 or so were men of obscure family, and they no doubt owed their prominence to proficiency in the severely Darwinian environment of the battlefield. At the end of the Middle Ages Nicholas Upton observed that service in the Hundred Years' War had enabled many 'poor men' to become noble. The picture should not, however, be overdrawn. The armies of the past were not run on meritocratic lines, and many embodied a particularly aggressive sense of hereditary privilege; but the honour code put a high value on the conspicuous display of courage under pressure. Nobles no doubt assumed easily enough that birth fostered such qualities. At the Estates-General of 1588, a spokesman for the French nobility told the king that their inherited 'generosity' committed them to serve the crown in war — and generosity was itself the mark of the *generosi*, the well-born. Yet if birth predisposed men to military distinction, the assumed connection could on occasion work the other way. Conspicuous prowess in arms, precisely because of its honourable associations, might entitle an individual to higher *social* standing than his origins strictly warranted. When William Robertson entered staff college in 1897, he was the first soldier from the ranks to have done so; he went on to become a field marshal — *and* acquire a baronetcy.

Not all recruits to the higher reaches of privilege entered via the battlefield. Civilian life had its own distinctions, and these too might suggest candidates for promotion to marks of honour. One obvious form of distinction was the acquisition of a large personal fortune. The relationship between wealth and rank, between money and aristocracy, was a persistently complex one, and in large part it forms the subject matter of the chapter which follows. Here we may simply note a continuing unease on the question. Should the successful entrepreneur — already by definition handsomely rewarded — acquire formal marks of public esteem? From the seventeenth century onwards, and perhaps earlier, economic writers attempted to persuade contemporaries that private wealth-creation indeed contributed to the public good; and that those who created it deserved corresponding recognition in the form of titles and privileges. But unease persisted nevertheless. Some fortunes had been made too fast, some men of business had displayed too shrewd an eye for gain, to make the grant of 'honours' generally acceptable. Feelings of this kind explain the hostility felt towards City merchants ennobled during the heyday of the Duke of Buckingham in the 1620s; and they may underlie the controversies provoked from time to time by recruitment to the contemporary British peerage.

Other civilian activities have proved less contentious, more widely accepted as a fitting route towards honour and privilege. Of these the most significant has been public service. In his *De Officiis* Cicero had argued that men could acquire as much honour in administering the affairs of the state as in fighting in its armies. The claim proved particularly attractive to the functionaries who staffed Europe's governmental systems. Whether the distinctive *éclat* of a military career was ever eclipsed is doubtful. (Doctor Johnson claimed that a man who had seen no active service was always likely to think 'meanly' of himself.) But public affairs enjoyed undoubted prestige. By the sixteenth century, senior office-holders in France and Spain had become entitled to such noble privilege as exemption from direct taxation. Men of long-standing noble ancestry thought it perfectly acceptable for their sons – their younger ones at any rate – to pursue a career in public administration. Prosperous merchants put their heirs through law schools as a down payment on future honours in government employment. Grimon Eyquem built a fortune on the waterfront of later fifteenth-century Bordeaux; his grandson worked as a royal magistrate before retiring to the countryside as 'Monsieur de Montaigne'.

Thus newcomers could acquire marks of honour and distinction. The privileged elite was duly replenished. In the language of Renaissance treatises on nobility, the claims of virtue and merit were added to those of birth. But this in no way undermined the importance of heredity: quite the reverse. For newcomers, honours represented only the start of a process of full ennoblement; the process required the passage of time for its competition. Individuals might stake a claim to new honours through gallantry in the field or devotion to the service of the state. Early in the sixteenth century, Castiglione advised the ambitious soldier to place himself in battle with a view to catching his captain's eye.

But the honours newly claimed were collective, not personal: to be carried on and enhanced by later generations. A gentleman could not be formed overnight, though kings might set the process in motion by granting title or privilege. (Proverbial wisdom had it that the only gentlemen created by a king were the sons of his own body.) As one generation followed the last, education and environment would do their work. A French commentator on army affairs wrote in 1787 that families recently granted privileges of nobility were likely to make excellent functionaries, even senior magistrates; only in the fourth generation should they receive the accolade of a military commission. In 1796 Edmund Burke's *Letter to a Noble Lord* warned his antagonist, the Duke of Bedford, not to brag about an ancestry of decidedly murky origins. But Burke was himself more alert than most to the potency of family honours inherited from the past; and to the hope that honours newly acquired might be passed on to future generations yet unborn. If heirs had survived him, Burke should himself have been 'a sort of founder of a family.' Past or future, honour was dynastic.

These considerations of honour and heredity are crucial to an understanding of what, until the very recent past, aristocracy has meant. High rank predisposed men to wield authority in all aspects of life, and the exercise of authority reinforced and enhanced that rank. Birth supplied old families with a distinctive, innate power of command; new arrivals hoped to transmit such authority to their descendants. When Friedrich Wilhelm IV of Prussia wrote Bismarck's letter of introduction to the Emperor Franz Josef, the king stressed ancient lineage as a principal indication of the minister's high qualities: 'he comes of a family settled in the eastern marches longer even than our own houses.' For the Greeks, aristocracy meant rule by the best. Throughout more recent times, it has meant rule by those whom birth placed high on the ladder of rank and status; and a concern with family and with hierarchy was to colour every aspect of aristocratic power. The following chapters will investigate some of the ways in which aristocratic leadership operated in practice. They will attempt to provide some explanation too for the hold which, down the centuries, aristocracy exercised over the rest of the community: and to suggest why, in the very long run, that hold has been broken.

2

Family and Fortune

Wealth and honour

Aristocracy implied wealth. Medieval chroniclers regularly named riches, along with ancestry and power, as the features which made great families truly distinctive. But the issue was complex. Did wealth in itself confer distinction ? And did distinctive hereditary rank assume that some forms of wealth-creation were appropriate to families of high status in a way that others were not?

In 1571 an Italian publicist named Muzio produced an attempt to answer these questions. Entitled *The Gentleman*, the work was dedicated to a well-born Venetian, Luigi Mocenigo; and the preface invoked Luigi's qualities in conventional terms: 'my natural Lord, most noble in ancestry, most illustrious in rank, and most outstanding in merit . . .' The flattery and the bombast make the point clearly enough: a Mocenigo was born to command others. Perhaps significantly, the preface avoids all reference to wealth. The text itself takes the form of a dialogue. Eugenio, a Florentine, guides a visitor, Nobile, round the sights of his native city. They pass a particularly fine palace, the property, as Eugenio explains, of 'a gentleman whose trading interests every day increase his fortune . . .' This provides Nobile's cue. Such an individual is clearly very rich, but is he a gentleman? Gentlemen are interested in material gain not for its own sake, but as a means to other, more public ends: charitable and educational spending, the construction of great buildings. Eugenio is able to claim that the ideal was more breached than observed: few men − however distinguished by birth or rank − actually lived like this. But Muzio's exceedingly unoriginal work leaves no doubt about what the ideal was. Birth placed men in a hierarchy of honour, and the enterprising individuals who rose from one rank to another passed that new rank on to their blood descendants. Forms of economic activity had their own hierarchy; some were compatible with high honourable rank, others less so. In 1858 the opening pages of Trollope's *Doctor Thorne* reminded readers that for all its utility, commerce could not be 'the noblest work of man'. In industrial England men of business were, of course, necessary, but they were not 'the first men among us'. Muzio's Nobile would have agreed. Aristocracy meant that some were born to wield authority over others, and to rank as 'the first men' in the community. And aristocratic economic life was profoundly shaped by considerations of what was honourable, compatible with this innate distinction, and what was not.

Long before Muzio, and more recently than Trollope, literary opinion doubted whether high rank could be based on commercial wealth. Did this view reflect the practice of everyday life? There will be more to say about the question in due course. What needs to be stressed here is that over the centuries one economic resource above all was associated with high aristocratic rank – land. In pre-industrial Europe, the economic importance of agrarian resource was obvious enough. But the speed and consistency with which liquid capital was sunk into country property suggests that more than purely economic considerations may have been at work. In the hinterland of great cities such as Venice or Barcelona, commercial wealth purchased rural estates – and merchant families turned themselves, with varying success at various periods, into noble ones. Countless marriage contracts stipulated that the money-gifts to the young couple go toward the acquisition of a landed estate. (In 1680 Louis XIV earmarked 800,000 *livres* for this purpose in the marriage negotiations of his natural daughter Marianne. The sum was regally colossal, but the thinking behind it was typical enough.) Land was distinctive. In part this was a matter of its security in comparison with other sources of revenue; though the balance of material advantage varied a good deal according to time and place. But land was distinctive, crucially, for the prestige and authority which attached to it. In contrast to other forms of property, the economist William Marshall pointed out in 1804, the landed estate carried its own peculiar 'dignity' and 'duties'.

This may get close to the heart of the connection between aristocracy and the land. Land was a capital asset, but it involved authority and a right of command as well. A Tudor antiquary

pointed out that the tribute money owed by inhabitants of the
Anglo-Welsh border to their Marcher barons represented not rent
but 'marks of lordship'. In a more remote past, indeed, land
would have been of small economic value had lords not exercised
coercive power over those who worked it. In systems of private or
feudal jurisdiction, 'lordship' – or more abrasive equivalents
such as *dominium* and *Herrschaft* – meant exacting labour services
from the tenantry, and inflicting due punishment on those who
resisted. The private franchises of the earlier Middle Ages were of
course gradually eroded. The slow – *very* slow – elaboration of
public institutions of justice and police meant that in the long run
the magnate would no longer be required to exercise personal
authority over those who worked his estates. Lordship was *en
route* to redefinition in more purely economic terms as landownership. But the countryside continued to abound in symbols of
distinctive privileges. In the 1760s Blackstone thought it outrageous that gentlemen, or their sons, or 'persons of superior
degree', should still enjoy a right to take game denied to humbler
countrymen. A hundred years on, Matthew Arnold's vision of an
aristocratic mansion as a 'great fortified post of the barbarians' no
doubt owed something to the polemical purposes of *Culture and
Anarchy*. But the image was not, in 1869, wholly fanciful: a
glimpse of the continuing power of heredity and privilege to
dominate an entire landscape.

Land was thus the aristocratic resource *par excellence*. Its
material value carried potent non-economic associations of
prestige and authority, and the character of aristocratic wealth is
incomprehensible without bearing those associations in mind.
This is particularly relevant to the question of aristocratic
patterns of expenditure. For noblemen to cut a figure with their
contemporaries, spending seems necessarily to have taken precedence over getting. This was a central point of Muzio's book;
for Nobile, mere acquisitiveness, the daily preoccupation with
earning more, was the hallmark of the merely rich. It was
spending, on such worthy causes as the foundation of schools or
financing the marriages of orphans, that distinguished the
gentleman. 'Generosity', in its original sense, was after all the
mark of the well-born. A good deal of the cultural history of the
West can be written in terms of aristocratic cash turned to lasting
and visible account. Three distinguished names taken more or

less at random − Balliol, Berry, Borghese − suggested objects as diverse as an Oxford college, an illuminated manuscript, and a villa set in a Roman garden. The 'generosity' of great families financed all three, and much else besides.

Aristocratic spending had more ephemeral uses too. Funerals provided a frequent occasion for conspicuous display, and both here and at less solemn moments lavish entertainment was to be expected. Hospitality and generosity went together. The Anglo-Saxon root of 'lord' had, after all, meant the leader who furnished his followers with bread. The association between big spending and a natural title may be of some significance. In the thirteenth century, Robert Grosseteste told the Countess of Lincoln that eating and drinking with his entourage was a sure way to build up the 'profit' and 'worship' of a great man. The tradition was a tenacious one. On the eve of the French Revolution, the highest-paid domestic in the Paris house of the Saulx-Tavannes family, Rue du Bac, was the Duke's chef, the appropriately named Monsieur Poisson. As late as 1863 an American visitor to Alnwick Castle was astonished at the scale of hospitality which the duke of Northumberland laid on for tenants and other locals; and he reflected that English aristocrats seemed brought up to take part in spectacular entertainment of this kind.

What did it all achieve? Over the centuries some observers sounded a sceptical note. The wiseacres of Tudor England had it that the only reward for a nobleman's good cheer was a 'great turd at his gate'. More decorous in expression, and in the long run more influential, were the promoters of efficiency and reform. In his travels around England during the 1760s and 1770s, Arthur Young noted − and deplored − the unwillingness of landowners to sacrifice the goodwill of their tenantry in pursuit of greater profits. Such advocacy of business method would gradually win the day over the traditions of conspicuous spending. But the very tenacity of that tradition over the centuries tells its own story. It may be that aristocratic investment in the visible, even the spectacular, brought returns of a kind. To the extent that great men were expected to display their greatness, those who did so were reminding contemporaries − and later generations − of their title to rank and authority.

The cost of generosity

But, inescapably, it all cost money. Sheer wealth – as writers on nobility tirelessly reminded their readers – was not in itself a social distinction. Yet to live like a family born to authority demanded the resources to spend like one. The fifteenth-century Spaniard Diego de Valera voiced a problem much discussed until comparatively recent times; too many men, he said, were accounted noble merely because they were rich, but too many titles were held by men 'unable to maintain their estate'. 'To maintain one's estate' was to enjoy the wealth which made conspicuous, lordly spending possible. In 1583, following this principle, the French government decreed that no one was to receive the title of duke who drew less than eight thousand gold crowns annually in landed revenues. Even after the First World War, Haig's elevation to the peerage provoked discussion about the financial resources appropriate to the rank of earl. Traditional ideas of 'generosity' lingered on.

The traditional nevertheless posed problems. Generosity, which included a readiness to spend conspicuously, was a mark of the *generosus*, the man of old, and distinguished, birth. But did birth automatically provide the means for such spending, the funds for banquets and funerals, for the construction of great houses and the commissioning of works of art? Clearly not. One of the most persistent features of the nobilities of the West has been the range of gradations within the privileged classes: from the more to the less grand, or fashionable, or powerful. There can be little doubt that disparities of wealth are an important element in the picture. As we have already seen, the different compensation rates which medieval Catalan custom allowed a viscount or a knight implied a close connection between rank and wealth. In the Brotherhood of the True Cross at Cáceres (Estremadura) at the end of the fifteenth century, *caballeros* were expected to make financial contributions double those asked of the less prestigious *hidalgos*.

Among the lower ranks of the privileged classes, in fact, a kind of relative (if rarely absolute) poverty must frequently have existed. In up-country Navarre the Marquis de Franclieu confided to his diary around the middle of the eighteenth century that he had been obliged to expel the resident tutor for seducing a maid; there was no question of his being able to afford a fashionable – and expensive – Paris college for any of his ten children. An anonymous English pamphlet of 1732 hinted at similar problems. Through the very fact of their birth, it argued, gentlemen of 'very ancient families' had a reputation to maintain, and often little enough to maintain it with; there were parks and houses to keep up and friends to entertain, and settlements to be made for daughters and younger sons. Indebtedness loomed. By this period, indeed, publicists and tidy-minded governments were devoting considerable attention to the question of 'poor nobles'. Hereditary privilege was associated in principle with the right and the duty to wield authority over others. So what justified the privileged status of families too poor to put those rights and duties into practice: too poor to purchase a commission in the king's armies, or serve in the administration of the state? By the time of the French Revolution, a number of solutions were on offer. Perhaps poorer nobles might be persuaded to overcome their prejudices, roll up their sleeves, and participate actively in trade or commerce. Or a quota of places might be reserved in regiments and military academies for the offspring of 'good' but needy families. The debate may in the longer run have done something to call into question the hereditary principle itself: to demystify the 'mysterious' potency traditionally attributed to blood and family. There will be more to say about this in due course. The point here is to establish poorer noble families as a kind of appendage to aristocracy. Birth conferred rank on the country gentleman as it did on the grandee and the magnate. All moved in the world of inherited privilege, and all were likely to regard land as the form of wealth most fitting to honourable rank. But the modest resources of a Marquis de Franclieu were the mark of a man remote from the more commanding forms of aristocratic power and prestige.

Great or small, however, noble fortunes shared certain characteristics. One was a tendency to incur debt. The aristocratic penchant for heavy borrowing has been a matter for contemporary comment down the centuries. For Renaissance moralists, debt was literally cancerous: the canker and ruin, in Francis Bacon's words, of many men's estates. When John Quincy Adams arrived in St Petersburg to represent the United States, he found a level of debt among the nobility of early nineteenth-century Russia that American opinion (he thought) would find dishonourable. Aristocratic debt has likewise impressed historians, and textbooks abound in references to the nemesis brought about by excessive borrowing. Noble extravagance emerges as a leading indicator of longer-term failure, and — through the mechanisms of debt — provides windfall profits for their more or less business-like creditors. Historians have been eager to analyse the 'crises' which have from time to time (allegedly) overtaken the nobilities of the West, and in their analyses the connection between debt and decline has featured strongly. Debt marks the route to the elephants' graveyard.

The argument is not wholly caricature. Borrowing was an occupational hazard among families of noble rank. Clarembaut de Atrive inherited one of the great fortunes of the fourteenth-century Netherlands, represented mainly by lands along the river Maas; but his reckless borrowing and spending reached such a pitch that in 1367 desperate members of his family had him killed. Here the problem of debt indeed threatened a whole noble lineage with disaster. But it may be that the Atrive case was an exceptionally extreme one. For many families, the management of debt appears to have been less critical and more chronic: and still less a threat to their position as leaders of the community. Historians have been inclined to regard debt as one of the means by which aristocratic authority was in the long run undermined by men with liquid capital to invest and to lend: by businessmen and entrepreneurs. But except for the very recent past, this view of things may verge on the anachronistic. In strongly hierarchical communities, the creditor of modest birth was likely to benefit from the patronage of the grandee to whom he lent. And not all lenders were men of modest birth. Among those who had made loans to the great Castilian house of Gandia in 1624, around half were wealthy city-dwellers (many with political affiliations to the Duke); the others were prominent nobles in their own right, a number of them Gandia kinsmen. The pattern was a familiar one, and it says a good deal about the character of aristocratic borrowing. Personal and family connections may have played as large a part as more purely market considerations in persuading creditors to place their cash. (And subsequent arguments over default or delayed repayment might become all the more rancorous as a result.) For aristocratic landowners, the need to borrow seems most often to have been a mark not of impending crisis, but of more or less awkward compromise.

A nobleman had to spend like one; he needed access, that is, to the funds required for marrying off a daughter, or burying a parent, in due style. 'Personal deficiencies in character and intelligence' – the severe phrase is Professor Lawrence Stone's – no doubt led individual noblemen into errors of judgement and fatal overcommitment. But the landed base of aristocratic fortunes imposed its own logic. Cash revenues were hard to predict: and property, as we shall see, was often hedged about by entails or other restrictions on an individual's capacity to realize capital assets. Until the very recent past, there were few facilities for the secure storage or banking of cash reserves. And the need to spend 'generously' was inescapable. So borrowing was hard to avoid. It represented an attempt to balance the needs of the moment against the inherited – and future – resources of the family as a whole. And over the centuries, debt was the process by which colossal sums of liquid cash were directed from a variety of sources towards that extremely aristocratic objective: less a sign of decline than a fact of life.

In part, therefore, the need to borrow reflected the need to spend. And in part it was a reflection of the character of noble fortunes, tied up as they predominantly were in buildings and land. But how were families to conserve, or even increase, those fortunes over the generations? Some noblemen were to display a striking readiness to invest in new forms of economic life – in agricultural, commercial, even industrial experiment – and there will be more to say about this later. But other routes towards wealth proved more consistently attractive. In the middle of the fifteenth century the Burgundian Gilbert de Lannoy warned his noble readers that riches must be acquired 'honourably,' and in his view no source of riches was more honourable than service to one's prince.

There was much in this. The previous chapter discussed some of the connections between service and social rank; a distinguished career in war or in public administration could take a newcomer (and his family) into the world of hereditary privilege, or advance him within it. And enhanced rank certainly implied wealth too. Service to the crown brought the Cecil family prestige and titles;

and it brought them the means to build Burghley and Hatfield as
well. Land as well as title rewarded the Conqueror's followers in
eleventh-century England, or those who fought for the house of
Trastámara in fourteenth-century Castile. But the link between
service and wealth was less direct than these success-stories might
suggest. Triumphs on the field of battle implied losers as well as
winners. Failure at court was less likely to be literally fatal, but
the favour of princes was notoriously as fickle as fortune's wheel.
The Hanoverian courtier Peregrine Bertie observed that the
profits of office were 'apples of Sodom': equally corrupting to
those who acquired them and to those who failed to do so. Men of
all ranks sought service with kings and grandees, and no doubt
hoped to gain materially in the process. But realists knew that it
was a chancy matter, and, as we shall see in due course, 'service'
implied a good deal more than a business arrangement.

Dynastic policy

One business arrangement above all others, however, offered
noble families down the centuries an opportunity to consolidate
and to extend their resources. This, of course, was marriage.
(Properly handled, Lannoy had pointed out in the fifteenth
century, marriage might prove as honourable and as profitable
as royal service or the spoils of war.) Not every consideration
could be precisely calculated in the course of a marriage
settlement; later events might turn satisfactory arrangements into
a disaster, or an unexpected treasure trove. It was in 1677 that
Mary Davies, twelve years old and heiress to the manor of Ebury,
married into the Grosvenor family; only in the course of the
following century did urban development begin to suggest the
colossal value which the London estate represented. But marriage
was nevertheless an opportunity for hard thought and (with luck)
for profit. Generation by generation, a family's inheritance was
subject to inevitable erosion as each principal heir made provision
for daughters and younger sons. The risky worlds of war and
politics might offer some sources of profit and so of compensation,
but nobles seem to have seen astute marriage as the principal key
to the problem. Early in the eighteenth century, a notary drew up a
kind of marital balance sheet for a branch of the great Venetian

house of Contarini. Over the past four generations, nine men of the family had married, and ten women; one more marriage portion, in other words, had been paid out than had come in. But the Contarini negotiators had done their work well. The men had received significantly larger portions than had been paid for the women, and the notary concluded that the arrangements taken as a whole left the family with a profit of 125,000 ducats.

Marriage had other purposes besides profit; or rather the rewards of a well-judged settlement could take forms other than cash or property. Families might enter negotiations out of long-standing friendships, or to cement a political alliance. By the eighteenth and nineteenth centuries, there were even signs that affection might provide suitable grounds for marriage: subject at any rate to parental approval. Overwhelmingly, however, these were collective arrangements, formulated and negotiated between families. Marriage contracts became increasingly elaborate documents; such devices as the English strict settlement, commonly met with from the later seventeenth century onward, defined not only the arrangements between the current families of bride and groom, but the disposal of property in the next generation as well. (An individual's will tended to be a far less elaborate affair. It might throw revealing light on the testator's state of mind, in the language employed or the charitable gifts ordered. But it was the contract of marriage which laid out the main lines for the descent of the estate.) When the Yorkshire gentleman Walter Calverley visited Newcastle in 1706 to discuss terms with his future mother-in-law, the negotiations − assisted by advice from friends and relatives on both sides − involved a three weeks' stay. As Montaigne pointed out, the individual got married: but at the heart of marriage was the family − in his word 'the posterity' − with its inheritance from the past and its hopes for the future.

Marriage provided an opportunity for new resources to enter a family estate; a shrewd eye for an heiress − like that apparently displayed by the Contarini − provided the means to go on living, and spending, nobly. But the significance of marriage ran deeper than that. Noble families who owed their rank to birth attached as much importance as any royal house to what might be called dynastic policy. And the primordial concern of all such policies was the survival of family and name. Extinction was after all a constant possibility. This probably explains why the Venetian nobleman Giovanni Donà decided to get married in 1711 at the age of forty-two. His first bride, a girl of sixteen, died in childbirth the following year; and Giovanni at once married again, going on to raise seven children. Giovanni's older brother had been married for eighteen years, but without heirs; no doubt the need to carry on the family name persuaded Giovanni to end his own long-standing bachelor status. Similar problems arose when a family continued only in the female line. Wills regularly stipulated that an heiress or a younger daughter was to receive her portion only on condition that any future husband take over the 'name and arms' of his father-in-law's family. It was this technique which enabled the distinguished Breton house of Montmorency to survive a failure of male heirs early in the fifteenth century.

Extinction was one threat. But fecundity raised its own problems too. An abundant family was in no immediate danger of seeing its 'name and arms' disappear, but provision for numerous children was always likely to impose serious strains on an estate. Around the middle of the fifteenth century, Diego Garcia de Ulloa was one of the most prominent noblemen of Cáceres in Estremadura; he had ten children – eight of them girls – and he saw them all married. Diego's liberal approach was probably exceptional: the mark of a particularly prosperous family at a time of conspicuous political success. Aristocratic practice in general seems to have been a good deal more restrictive. In each generation a principal heir could expect to enjoy the bulk of the estate; younger brothers less or nothing; and where daughters were numerous, marriage for some only. (The tendency for so many Venetian noblemen to remain single, as in the Donà case discussed earlier, probably reflected the need to avoid fragmenting the family fortune.) Already in the earlier Middle Ages, legal devices such as the *melioratio* enabled one or two sons to concentrate the lion's share of the estate in their hands. This may have owed something to factors other than economic ones; where a noble inheritance meant a castle as well as land, it no doubt made military sense to vest authority in one clearly designated commander. But the practice of concentrating a family's resources long outlasted the days of knights and castellans. When Jacques de Saulx-Tavannes inherited his Burgundian estates early in the seventeenth century, this represented two-thirds of the family's patrimony as a whole. The remaining one-third met the needs of Jacques' younger siblings: ten of them. A married sister received a marriage-portion in cash; small landed properties went to two married brothers; two other brothers died unmarried; the rest entered the church.

Practices of this kind reveal a good deal about aristocratic attitudes: attitudes both towards wealth and towards the family. The individual, whether favoured or excluded in the transmission of the estate from one generation to the next, was under pressure. The social and psychological results of such pressure are in large part a matter for historical speculation. The cult of chivalry, for instance, has been associated with the problems of aristocratic younger sons: excluded from wealth by dynastic policies which in the twelfth and thirteenth centuries increasingly concentrated estates in the hands of a single heir, they were hence forced to try their fortune in private warfare or on crusade. Early in the fifteenth century, the first earl of Westmorland added to the tensions of contemporary politics by disinheriting his eldest son in favour of the children of his ambitious second wife Joan Beaufort. As to what the younger brothers and sisters of Jean de Saulx-Tavannes thought of the arrangements described above, we simply do not know.

So the family – past, present, future – came first: a principle heavy with consequences for the individuals who composed it. The ruthless behaviour which this on occasion involved may have a wider bearing on the economic activities of aristocrats in general. It may be true that aristocratic culture implied the pre-eminence of spending over getting: of resources made visible and enacted in feasts and funerals, or transmitted over the generations in buildings and land. But resources had to come from somewhere. This, after all, dictated the frequently harsh logic of marriage and inheritance. The same consideration forced many nobles towards a perhaps unexpected concern with sound financial management. 'Keep your pocket-book steady', Lord Ashburnham advised his son when the young man was administering the family's Sussex estates at the beginning of the eighteenth century. Not all nobles heeded this wise counsel, but its validity in principle won general acceptance.

'Thrift' was, of course, not an aristocratic watchword, and the notion of living 'nobly' or 'like a gentleman' – as we have seen –

easily eclipsed the attractions of sheer profiteering. The landed base of so much aristocratic wealth added to the problems of efficient business management. Scattered properties made accurate accounting difficult, and much no doubt turned on the relations between individual nobles and their local agents. 'I must have detail and exactness in all your undertakings: you write me nothing but monosyllables,' a Gascon landowner complained to his steward in 1772. Detailed and exact accounting might be hard to achieve; but it provided the resources for an authentically aristocratic style of living.

Historians have sometimes associated this attention to financial detail with the spread of 'new' attitudes among the nobility: attitudes variously described — and at a variety of periods — as bourgeois or capitalistic. This is probably misleading. Shrewdness, and greed, are human characteristics rather than those of a class; and there is no reason to suppose that Mr Gradgrind possessed them in fuller measure than a Victorian peer. The point is rather that nobles exploited their resources, with greater or lesser efficiency, for their own distinctively aristocratic purpose. When the Venetian noble Leonardo Donà drew up his accounts in 1611, he noted his long-standing practice of monthly saving and his careful avoidance of personal pleasures: a salute to method and frugality. But to what end? Donà couched his objective in the most explicitly aristocratic terms: his carefully accumulated fortune was to purchase a landed estate 'proper to the station and reputation of my future heirs'.

For earlier periods such direct evidence becomes more elusive. But we can surmise that then, as later, successful noble families used hard-headed (and sometimes heavy-handed) methods to maintain their aristocratic standing. In the late fourteenth and fifteenth centuries, English landowners had to adjust to the complex long-term consequences of the Black Death: tenurial confusion, falling demand for rural produce, a depleted labour force. Yet in the main the storm was weathered. And the leading authority in the matter concludes that — a few spectacular failures apart — it was 'harsh efficiency' that saw noble families through. Early in the sixteenth century, the third Stafford Duke of Buckingham became a by-word for aristocratic ambition in the grand style: for his great lordships in the Welsh marches, for his lavish building-schemes at Thornbury, and for the (obscure)

political designs which took him to the block in 1521. Among his
tenantry, the Duke's name stood rather differently: as a ruthless
landlord whose exactions were administered by an energetic team
of stewards, commissioners, and casual informers. The duke's
spectacular rise and fall epitomized a more general aristocratic
concern with visible pre-eminence in the community. Public
distinction of this kind in turn depended on the shrewd
harnessing of resources: whether in arranging marriages or in
managing the estates. And on occasion 'shrewd' might properly
be replaced by harsher adjectives.

Aristocratic property, old and new

So alertness was crucial. Aristocratic success was not to be judged
in purely economic terms, but it was incompatible with economic
failure. Over the centuries, the material resources of great
families meant above all else land and the family. But new forms
of economic activity provided new opportunities. And nobles
were from time to time to prove as alert in venturing into overseas
trade – or town planning, or industrial development – as in
exploring their estates and ordering their family affairs. In the
early seventeenth century, such grandees as the Earls of
Southampton and Bedford took a leading part in the fashionable
(and profitable) building schemes which increasingly linked
Westminster to the City of London. By the middle of the
eighteenth century, French trading companies in Guyana or the
Baltic could count on the participation both of prominent
courtiers and of respectable country gentlemen. And when
around the same period progressive Spanish publicists sought an
example of the benefits to be derived from industrial enterprise, it
was to the career of the Basque nobleman (and manufacturer)
Juan de Goyeneche that they pointed.

Where aristocracies survived into the nineteenth century, they
continued to benefit from participation in new forms of enterprise. Recent research has suggested that the support of such men
as the Earls of Dudley and Dartmouth, with their extensive Black
Country property, helped to shape urban and industrial development in the West Midlands. The princely families of Fürstenberg
and Schwarzenberg added their prestige to the name of Credit-

Anstalt when that great Viennese finance house opened in 1855. And when Lord Randolph Churchill — third son of a duke — speculated on young Winston's future in the event of his rejection by Sandhurst, it was to a career in the City that he looked. Aristocracy implied no necessary hostility to new and sometimes spectacular sources of wealth.

But the subject nevertheless remained a complex one. Old suspicions about too-direct involvement in trade (let alone manual labour) lingered on down the centuries, as Trollope's words reminded us early in this chapter. Commerce was indeed useful, but in no sense 'man's noblest work'. When Lord Mountjoy became heavily involved in the running of his alum works at Canford, early in the reign of Elizabeth, his neighbours murmured that he was turning from a gentleman into a miner. The whole point about the commercial or industrial activities described above was that the aristocratic involvement remained a matter of participation at arm's length. Cash investment, sympathy, even a measure of overall direction: noble backing could provide all these. Yet motives behind such backing were probably mixed. Nobles were hardly immune from hopes of profit; birth no doubt appeared to confer a right (and duty) to leadership in this as in other walks of life; and some nobles may have been attracted by the risk. But the detail of day-to-day commercial or industrial management was most appropriately left to others. By the time of the enlightenment, it is true, some bold spirits were attempting to challenge ancient prejudices in the name of prosperity and public utility. What mattered was the creation of wealth, the critics argued, not the social rank of those who created it, nor the social esteem attaching to particular forms of wealth-creation: let nobles participate directly in all manner of trade and manufacture, let successful entrepreneurs be accounted nobles for their success. Yet even in the eighteenth century, old prejudice was to die hard. Aristocratic fortunes might tap new resources, but they did so in distinctively aristocratic fashion. Nobles were (innately) different; their economic activity must conform to that fundamental premise. When Juan de Goyeneche died in 1735, his industrial concerns had made him a hero to enlightened opinion. But their disposal proved no less significant. The industrial holdings passed to his sons with the rest of his estate in the classic Spanish aristocratic form of the *mayorazgo:* not as a marketable asset, but joined in perpetuity to the patrimony of future generations of Goyeneche. New forms of wealth appeared; aristocratic attitudes towards their use proved slower to change.

Goyeneche's disposal of his estate suggests in a general way the tenacity of old views of family and property. (For a man who spent the last years of his life getting his sons admitted to the military orders of Spain − the ancient crusading brotherhoods of Santiago and Calatrava − this conservatism is hardly surprising.) And there may be a more specific point at issue. In 1735 the celebrated nobleman/entrepreneur passed on his property to future generations of the family. But we have to understand 'property' in a highly distinctive, and aristocratic, sense. Goyeneche's rank empowered him to set up a *mayorazgo* or entail. Once entailed, his estate was in principle sealed off from the forces of the market, whatever the financial pressures on a future heir, or the hopes of potential purchaser. Privilege shaped property in all its aspects. High status might entitle those who enjoyed it to make acquisitions from which others were debarred; and an arrangement like Goyeneche's entail could prevent an heir from exercising absolute control over his estate. Marx once pointed to what he called the 'indeterminate' character of property as the term had been understood throughout much of the European past. It was hereditary status which did much to keep the concept blurred.

A good deal has already been said about the role of land in aristocratic fortunes, about land as the aristocratic resource *par excellence*. In part this reflects its economic significance in pre-industrial times; but as we have already seen, the large-scale ownership of land carried with it powerful traditional associations with command and lordship. These no doubt enhanced the dignity of the landowner, but they may also have suggested that landownership was itself properly the preserve of men born to command − that is, hereditary nobles. The old feudal tag 'no land without a lord' could certainly be taken in this sense. In a number of European countries, the later Middle Ages saw attempts to enforce the principle that only men of noble stock could acquire landed estates. Devices such as the French tax of *francs-fiefs* sought to maintain the tradition: while tacitly admitting that large numbers of wealthy commoners (who paid the tax) were in practice buying their way into rural property. Where the economy was less advanced, cash made its inroads more slowly, and the restriction of landownership to those of high rank retained its hold longer. In Silesia at the end of the eighteenth century, 1,200 noble families owned manors while only 200 families of townspeople did so. In Western Europe by that period, questions of status had become largely detached from the workings of the land-market; vendor and purchaser, whatever their rank, dealt (literally) in the same currency. Some aspects of landownership nevertheless retained their associations with hereditary status. In the reign of George IV, a Bedfordshire magistrate deplored a poacher's casual way with the rights of 'private property'. Yet English law interpreted these rights of property in a distinctive and revealing fashion. The legitimate taking of game, infringed by the poacher, was confined to gentlemen and substantial freeholders. This excluded the poor; and it also kept out the 'merely' wealthy with liquid assets but no land. Hence, in 1827, Lord Londonderry's observation on the peculiar − that is, aristocratic − pleasure of sending game to one's friends: 'nobody would care for a present which everbody could give.' Only in the course of the nineteenth century did law reform strip these privileges away. The pursuit of game was to become the pastime of those who could afford it. And so one understanding of property very gradually gave way to another.

Londonderry's comment implied an exclusiveness of birth which coloured traditional views of property. The aristocratic monopoly over game echoes a more distant past when land-ownership itself had been the preserve of the well-born. For those of a rank to enjoy it, landed property traditionally implied not only a material resource but prestige and perhaps privilege too. As Archdeacon Grantly pointed out, an estate brought its owner influence and position as well as rents: 'to say nothing of the game'. Aristocratic property suggested rights rather more extensive than the possession of a piece of land.

But in certain circumstances it might also suggest something rather less. As we have seen, aristocratic fortunes were essentially family fortunes. How much freedom could the family allow an individual nobleman in handling the 'property' which he 'owned'? The entail which Juan de Goyeneche placed on his estate, industrial holdings included, is one example of a classic aristocratic response to the problem. From the late Middle Ages on, entail or its equivalents – *mayorazgo*, or *fideicommissum* – became a familiar part of the legal system of Western Europe. These devices kept the partimony as a whole intact by placing some (or all) of it beyond the free disposal of the current head of the family: hence the necessity for borrowing to meet immediate cash needs. In the absence of such formal restrictions, the noble landowner might nevertheless think it necessary or politic to submit his financial arrangements to the scrutiny of 'family and friends'. The formula is abundantly cited in notarized documents; a particularly elaborate example, including a number of cousins, concerns the consultations carried out by Pierre de Montaigne in making plans for the marriage of his son, the essayist Michel, in 1567. In some regional customs, kinsmen had a right – within defined time-limits – to intervene in the sale of land between members of their family and any third party. And in some parts of Europe, notably Scandinavia, traditions of kin-punishment lingered on into the sixteenth century, if not later: a landowner might be called on to pay cash or donate goods in compensation for the misdeeds of a kinsman.

So the collective interest of the larger family pressed in on concepts of individual property ownership. Other traditional patterns of thought and behaviour worked in the same direction. In the great codifications of feudal law which were undertaken in so much of Western Europe during the thirteenth century, the point was made particularly clear: where a man (and this regularly meant a noble) held land by homage to a superior, he must neither sell nor engage that land without his superior's consent. What place was there here for an individual's absolute right of ownership? Over time, of course, this classic expression of feudal hierarchy gradually lost much of its relevance. The powers of the superior lapsed, or turned into a commodity bought and sold for cash. Yet ancient rights enjoyed a tenacious after-life, even when apparently forgotten. Magnates of the highest rank could find the enjoyment of their property under sudden threat in the name of 'feudal' dues. In the years after 1627 a particularly energetic agent for the Earl of Salisbury set out to establish the feudal rights which his master could claim from tenants on the West Country estates. Archival research provided the basis for a number of successful actions by the Earl as feudal superior; substantial sums were paid to him by tenants who included prominent local gentlemen and the Earl of Suffolk. On the Continent, rights such as these — a lord's wardship over a tenant's minor heir, his power to impose cash fines when a new tenant inherited — probably remained more extensive, and more energetically enforced, than in England. On the eve of the French Revolution, a trade directory informed the landowners of Languedoc that in the city of Toulouse alone they could choose from eleven specialists in the pursuit of feudal rights. But the successful assertion of one man's claim meant the erosion of another's property. And high rank was no necessary protection. In 1746 the Baron de Montesquieu's plan to purchase a farmstead adjoining one of his country properties came to an abrupt end; a neighbour, the Marquis d'Escouloubre, pre-empted the deal by asserting feudal rights over the property concerned. Montesquieu was no novice in legal affairs, whether as former magistrate or as the author of *The Spirit of the Laws* (published two years later). But on this occasion the great man found himself hopelessly wrong-footed. In a letter to the Marquis he deplored the use of a device which would have been sharp practice 'even against one of your most wretched *bourgeois*'. But 'between people such as ourselves . . . who have the honour to be neighbours, and bound by so many ties of family', the thing was quite outrageous.

Trivial in itself, Montesquieu's discomfiture in 1746 may have some wider significance. The letter to the Marquis could scarcely have sounded a more aristocratic note: 'honour' and 'family' are as central to it as to the long sections on nobility in *The Spirit of the Laws* itself. But Montesquieu's outrage was the outrage of a property-owner as well as of a gentleman. A claim based on dusty feudal rights had forced him to abort a promising market transaction. Property rights in the matter had favoured ancient noble custom at the expense of the ownership conferred by purchase. The advantages represented by certain traditional forms of property — feudal privilege among them — might thus make other forms dangerously precarious. Considerations of this sort no doubt help to explain the growing campaign against such rights in the course of the eighteenth century. Noble landowners themselves came to appreciate the benefits of resolving the indeterminate character of property ownership: of making that ownership absolute, irrespective of the owner's status or of the nature of the thing owned. Root out feudal rights, the moderate deputy Martinez de la Rosa told the Spanish Cortes in 1811, and the solid trunk of property will be all the better secured. But the consequences for aristocracy were to be momentous nevertheless, as the final chapter will suggest. If the concept of property had traditionally been a fluid and uncertain one, it was because the term was shot through by considerations of rank and birth. There were forms of property − most notably land − which were associated with high descent and an authority greater than the capital value of the estate. Some kinds of property were intrinsically special; just as some kinds of people were themselves naturally ('by birth') special too. The point can be applied to aristocratic economic activity as a whole. Innately different, nobles made money and spent it and passed on their fortunes in ways which made that difference manifest. But what if that innate difference were denied? What if each individual were freed from 'the obstacles which have hitherto hindered them' in the pursuit of prosperity? (This was the wording of the Prussian decree of 1807 which abolished serfdom and other seigneurial powers.) And what if this 'prosperity' might be embodied in property of any kind − irrespective of the traditional pre-eminence of land? (On this matter the Prussian legislators were silent.) An increasing attention to the absolute character of individual property rights raised both questions directly. An unequal society was elaborating a new organizing principle: the equal right of each individual to pursue wealth in whatever way he chose. And what would become of aristocracy then?

3

The Power of Command

Aristocracy and leadership

In 1863 a newly created baronet, Francis Crossley, bought the substantial country property of Somerleyton in Suffolk. Crossley was not a native East Anglian; he came from Halifax in the West Riding of Yorkshire, where his family had made a fortune in the manufacture of carpets. The sales particulars described Somerleyton as an estate ideally suited 'to the requirements of a nobleman, or gentleman of taste and fortune', comprising house, wintergarden and four thousand acres. But there was more besides. There were 'extensive manors or lordships with all the rights, privileges and emoluments appertaining thereto'; and there was the power to appoint an incumbent for the village church. By 1863, language of this kind was no doubt consciously loaded. On the Victorian property market, an evocation of the medieval and the picturesque was likely to make good business sense. Crossley's story nevertheless points up the immense and continuing appeal of aristocracy: and of those aristocratic attitudes and patterns of behaviour discussed in previous chapters. His baronetcy promised a distinctive hereditary rank for future generations of the family. Somerleyton embodied the attractions of a distinctive kind of investment. And in his new 'lordships' and church patronage, Crossley acquired, in however attenuated a form, rights even more essential to the character of aristocracy: symbols of one man's power to command others.

For the Greeks, 'aristocracy' meant a specific form of government. More recent usage has shifted towards those who rule. In either sense the element of command is inescapable. F. W. Maitland thought it wrong to describe medieval peasants as their lord's tenants: 'subjects' would be a better term. Whatever the word used, the reality of aristocratic lordship was often enough a harsh one. The Flemish chronicler Galbert of Bruges wrote early in the twelfth century that greed and cruelty were the vices peculiar to knights and barons; around the same period, the historian Orderic Vitalis described the Norman magnates settled in post-conquest England as mere 'foreign robbers'. Seven centuries on, in 1837, Richard Cobden attacked the landed interest by recalling the barbarity of the medieval baronage, and by pointing to current ill-treatment of rural labourers at the hands of their aristocratic employers: 'I almost said their owners.' Not surprisingly, such hostility has found an echo in recent historical writing. As we have already seen, the study of aristocracy has often sat uneasily with the great themes of nineteenth- and twentieth-century scholarship: with the rise of the national state, or of the middle class, or of the masses. 'Feudal anarchy', or 'aristocratic oppression', have bulked large, and not wholly without reason. J. P. Poly has recently described the extension of seigneurial authority over the free peasantry of eleventh and twelfth century Provence as a process of 'class terror'. And it was coercion, so it has been argued, which provided the ultimate basis for the apparent calm of aristocratic rule in Hanoverian England.

There will be more to say about such analyses in due course. *Some* link between aristocracy and coercive force is hardly to be denied. The nobilities of the West were heirs to the mounted warriors – the *bellatores* – of the high Middle Ages. The sword which signified a man's capacity 'to give satisfaction' was also a mark of power. At the height of Venetian influence in the fifteenth and sixteenth centuries, young patricians regularly wielded naval or military command in the eastern Mediterranean before returning to the Republic in pursuit of a civilian career. And the laws which over so much of Westen Europe kept hunting a noble monopoly frequently made the military association quite explicit: in the chase, gentlemen learned the discipline and dash necessary for battlefield command. (The career of the Marquis of Granby, commemorated by scores of public houses, is a case in point. The celebrated master of foxhounds – with the Belvoir – saw action at Minden and Warburg before becoming Commander-in-Chief in 1766.)

For better or worse, aristocratic leadership carried potent associations with sheer force, on or off the field of battle. But this was not the whole story. For all its influence and prestige, the profession of arms was only one among several expressions of aristocratic authority. In twelfth-century Flanders, Galbert of Bruges had deplored the excesses of noblemen, but their violence and rapacity seemed to him the characteristic failings of a natural ruling class. That rule took two forms: bearing arms (for protecting the poor and the church) and giving counsel to the prince. This was the ideal, as Galbert no doubt recognized. Whatever the gap between ideal and reality, 'the giving of counsel' was nevertheless long taken as a prime expression of aristocratic power and responsibility. Long before Galbert's time, the great men of the Carolingian Empire had sworn to give aid and counsel to Charlemagne and his heirs. Such phrases became stock items in the terminology of feudal contracts. And when by the end of the thirteenth century 'parliaments' were meeting with increasing frequency at Westminster and elsewhere, it was in terms of their duty to give counsel that English kings such as Edward I summoned their greatest subjects to appear.

'Giving counsel' is a convenient medieval shorthand. It might be reworded to suggest engagement and leadership in public life generally. In the ancient world, Cicero had seen distinction in the life of the community as fully comparable to the glory earned on the battlefield. In the later Middle Ages and beyond, the activities of government expanded, the opportunities for civilian distinction grew apace, and Cicero's dictum took on particular relevance. 'I put aside the lance to take up the pen' was the observation of the Burgundian authority on chivalry, Olivier de la Marche, when he engaged in secret diplomacy on his ducal master's behalf early in the 1470s. 'The pen' no doubt symbolized the important public duties of the kind that Cicero had envisaged long before. But the phrase had another significance. How did the training which nobles received measure up to the demands of *literate* leadership?

Historians have not in the main been much impressed by standards of aristocratic learning. It may be that members of a hereditary elite are less likely than ambitious newcomers to gravitate to the forefront of intellectual enquiry. An excess of book-learning has traditionally met with aristocratic disdain. Men of standing need common sense and judgement, said Montaigne, not the pedantry of scholars. Perhaps so. But this was an author writing with publication in view; he was, even by the standards of the sixteenth century, a crashing snob; and he had received a superb training in Latin. The third Earl Grey was a good deal more direct when he gave evidence to the Army Commissioners in 1857; he opposed introducing academic selection for military candidates, he explained, because French experiments in the matter had led to 'a very serious increase of brain disease among the young'. An education at Eton and Trinity, Cambridge, had clearly left the Earl with a proper scepticism about the claims of paper qualifications.

The subject of education is in any case a tricky one. Only a few years before the enquiry of 1857, a British commander had thought Latin a suitable cypher in which to signal a new acquisition for the crown. (Napier's '*Peccavi*: I have Sind', followed the capture of that territory in 1843.) Born leaders had little need for erudition, but far back into the Middle Ages leadership had been associated with wisdom, prudence, and a wide general knowledge. 'Sage' Oliver, after all, was a leading hero of chivalry. The inheritance of classical antiquity made it hard to divorce the business of command from the rational calculations of the commanders. Sheer force was hardly adequate, and if nobles lacked the wit to rule, there were no doubt others ready to replace them. In the middle of the fifteenth century, Gomez Manrique, brother of the Master of Santiago, told his fellow nobles of Castile to study how the ancients governed the Roman state if they were to continue running theirs. As opportunities for formal education expanded during and after the Renaissance, Gomez' advice was widely followed. New schools and colleges were founded, and often with the needs of the deserving and disadvantaged in mind. Their subsequent development frequently suggests a rather different story. The foundation of Eton made provision for the maintenance of 'thirteen poor men', but they disappear from the later fifteenth century records. By the eve of the English Civil War, the school could boast an impressive tally of earls' sons. The educational demands of high public office continued to rise, but the process of aristocratic adaptation continued likewise. When competitive entrance examinations were introduced as part of the mid-nineteenth century reform of the British civil service, many feared social upheaval. Gladstone disagreed. He predicted that such rigours would confer nothing but advantages on 'gentlemen by birth and training'. And as it turned out, he was right. In the early years of the present century, entrants to the top stream of the Diplomatic

Service were required to demonstrate academic competence; to enjoy a private income; and to receive the endorsement of 'men of standing and position' known personally to the Foreign Secretary. Training for leadership evolved over the centuries, but leadership remained a business for gentlemen.

The birthright of power

Prominence in public affairs was thus long associated with distinctive and inherited rank. 'Men of standing and position' provided natural leaders in all fields. Leadership might mean command in battle; it might mean high civil office; it might, as the preceding chapter suggested, imply an aristocratic readiness to invest in new areas of economic activity. And to these varying demands, the education of nobles responded with varying degrees of success. But was there anything distinctively aristocratic in all this? A wideranging power of command may characterize ruling classes where no aristocracy exists. Some analysts of advanced societies in the West have discerned a 'power elite' whose members wield decisive influence over all aspects of public affairs. In the less reputable 'authoritarian' regimes of the developing world, small groups of families play a disproportionate role in politics, business and the army. Something of the kind may also be true (more discreetly) of the privileged classes of Eastern Europe. If aristocracy implies a general presumption of one group's leadership in the community, it may be useful to say rather more about the distinctively aristocratic forms which that leadership took.

One thing that mattered was place. As the characteristics of feudal lordship begin to emerge from the patchy documentation of the early Middle Ages, noble authority meant above all else power over land and those who peopled it. That power was made visible in stone. A monastic document from the Bordeaux region spoke in 1087 of 'the great men of the province, those who own castles'. Over the generations, castles and land bound families to their locality. German historians write of the *Stammsitz*, the family seat, from which even modest noble families increasingly took their name. The aristocratic association with a *particular* locality long outlived the military role of the castle. The great patrician families of Florence or Venice had their own neighbourhoods where their palaces, and the bulk of their kinsmen and followers, were to be found. Local connection permeated the political world in which nobles exercised their authority. When Lord Powis petitioned ministers on behalf of 'my countrymen' in the 1750s, he meant his 'Shropshire friends': clients and assorted hangers-on from the county in which so much of his power was based.

Great men were the natural leaders of their local community. Over time, local connection reinforced the innate character of aristocratic authority. As we have seen, newcomers were constantly recruited into the ranks of the privileged, but the passage of time added a distinction of its own. And time coloured aristocratic power as it did aristocratic status. When a Provençal noblewoman recorded her claims to authority over the smallholders of the Carmargue at some date around 1060, it was in terms of 'customs' and 'long usage' that she did so. Max Weber thought that until the very recent past, the wielding of power was a kind of innate distinction – *Eigenwürde* – vested in particular families and individuals. Something of the sort applies to aristocracy. The 'customary' authority invoked by the Provençal noblewomen was in the most proprietary sense hers (or her family's): not provisional or delegated. Indeed the more rigorous theorists in these matters would often reject 'privilege' as a term to describe aristocratic rank or power. Privilege implied a grant or concession by higher authority; and this was hardly appropriate to people whose claim to authority rested on who they were.

More precisely, that claim rested on who their forebears were. 'Innate' authority implies hereditary authority. The first chapter suggested that assumptions about heredity dominated ideas on noble status. The same is true of aristocratic power. Distinctive birth implied taking a lead in public affairs. The young Disraeli thought this one of the great strengths of English political life. Hereditary leadership was most obviously embodied in the House of Lords; but he observed that in the Commons too, members were regularly drawn from among 'the first families of the shires', to the satisfaction of the public in general. Respect for hereditary power may by this date (1835) have become less universal than Disraeli claimed. But the connection between high birth and public authority had over the centuries proved an immensely tenacious one. In the eleventh or twelfth centuries, 'the great men who owned castles' owed that power in the main to inheritance from their fathers. Authority of a different kind, embodied in Charlemagne and his successors, had once claimed to make local aristocratic influence conditional on loyal service to the Empire. And as we shall see, that claim — in the name of 'the public good' or, increasingly, of 'the state' — was to be heard again in later centuries. But well before the year 1000, the institutions of the Empire had largely crumbled away, and local power for better or worse had reverted into the hands of the *castellani* and their heirs. The great territorial clans of medieval Catalonia, the Cabrera, the Cardona, the Rocaberti, owed their initial advance to service as 'vicars' or lieutenants of the Count of Barcelona; but the Count's power dwindled, and theirs became ancestral. This link between heredity and leadership survived to find an echo in Disraeli's day. And it could be taken as axiomatic, too, among the families which governed the great cities of Renaissance Europe. Early in the sixteenth century, the historian and diplomat Francesco Guicciardini proclaimed two objectives for his literary and political activity: to defend the liberty of his native Florence, and to maintain 'the renown of the house of Guicciardini, not only while I live, but for all time'. The two aims were complementary. A public role was part of the aristocrat's inheritance.

Not only did great families inherit a power of command over others; the institution of the family itself provided a setting and an idiom in which command could be exercised. Until the very recent past, parents could invoke the fifth commandment as the first stage in a chain of obedience which culminated in the authority of God Himself. Children of all classes were, of course, urged to honour their fathers and mothers. But the head of an aristocratic household enjoyed exceptional resources with which to assert both the distinction of his house and his own role as its leader. Much of the conspicuous expenditure discussed in the previous chapter can be linked to the pursuit of these objectives. As Grosseteste had pointed out in the course of the thirteenth century, nothing better marked out the pre-eminence of a great lord than to dispense lavish entertainment for his kinsmen and followers. When the Duke of Berry commissioned his celebrated *Book of Hours* around 1410, one illustration would depict him in a banquet-setting of just this kind: the grandee presiding over the sumptuous conviviality of his household at table.

Leadership in the community was the birthright of great aristocratic lineages. And in each generation the embodiment of that authority, both public and domestic, was the head of the family. Religious imagery drove the point home. In 1528 Titian completed a *Madonna* to commemorate the recent victory of the Venetian nobleman Jacopo Pesaro in naval war against the Turks. The painting, in the Franciscan church of Santa Maria, duly notes the achievements of the individual and the distinction of his house as a whole: an attendant stands guard over a captive Turk, and holds aloft the heraldic Pesaro banner. Jacopo, the victorious commander, is the scene's principal human figure. He alone looks directly at the Virgin, and the upward diagonal of his gaze provides the key to Titian's overall design. The rest of the family have their eyes on Jacopo, their leader and representative before the Mother of God. Yet for all its suggestion of patriarchal authority, the work clearly concerns the house of Pesaro in its entirety. Heraldic images evoke a distinguished ancestry; Virgin and attendant saints promise intercession for Jacopo and his kinsmen; and the work was doubtless designed to stimulate the devotions of later generations of the Pesaro line. The *Madonna* links a great noble's domestic authority as head of the family to his public achievement as commander in war. And it relates them both to the fortunes of a whole lineage: past, future and beyond the grave.

Religion provided extensive opportunities for displaying these distinctively aristocratic concerns. Funerals were especially apt. When a prominent magistrate and landowner died at Bordeaux in 1563, his body was transported up river to his estate on the Dordogne; carried in procession with twenty-five of the parish poor (one of whom displayed his scarlet robes of office); and buried in his ancestors' chapel of 'Monseigneur St. Front', patron saint of the province. An event of this kind gave visible form to some important characteristics of aristocratic authority. This was a man born to command others, and it was appropriate enough that after death he returned to the ancestral place which had given him that title to leadership. There were many larger aristocratic fortunes than his, and the funerals of the very great demonstrated their commanding authority in correspondingly lavish fashion. Processions, elaborate funerary monuments, colossal bouts of eating and drinking, heraldic display: down the centuries,

aristocratic interments were marked by all these. Moralists
constantly deplored the association of a Christian's departure with
these scenes of atavistic extravagance. One Elizabethan observed
that too many peers were buried as if they had been 'Duke Hector
. . . or Sir Launcelot'. But the imagery of rank and authority
remained intensely potent. The grandee went to his resting-place
less as the individual of distinction than as the conspicuous
embodiment of hereditary power. In the arrangements which the
Scottish heralds drew up for the funerals of peers early in the
seventeenth century, heredity and leadership received their full
due. Marchers in the procession were to carry the family's arms,
back to the great-grandparents of the deceased; a lackey guided
the great horse on which the peer had ridden to Parliament; and
another carried those symbols of rank, 'his arming sworde with
his spurres'. The man was dead; but in the colour and pomp of
funeral display the family's claim to leadership lived on.

Friends and followers

In all these matters, 'family' may often have extended some way
beyond the strict bounds of blood kinship. The Scottish heralds
planned that large numbers of 'followers' should take part in the
funeral procession of their dead lord, and it was no doubt
assumed that some of these had formed part of his domestic
establishment. Far back into the Middle Ages, the archives of
royal households throughout Western Europe, and of the greater
magnates too, record the presence of 'bachelors' in the leader's
entourage. The term — like 'vassal' or 'knight' — originally
implied youth, and the immense authority and prestige embodied
in the household of a great man presumably encouraged
ambitious young nobles to attach themselves for a time to his
'family'. Over much of Western Europe, this function of the
household was gradually losing its significance by the end of the
Middle Ages; formal educational institutions — schools, colleges
— increasingly took their place in a noble's *curriculum vitae*. But the
family stood inescapably at the centre of aristocratic power. And to
associate oneself with the head of a great lineage — whether as
equal or as subordinate — was to enter a relationship which had
something in common with the blood tie itself.

In 1368, for instance, the Lord of Wildenburg agreed to take service with the Count of Flanders in all his affairs. The Count paid Wildenburg fifty crowns, which Wildenburg duly, and in 'friendly' fashion (*vriendelike*), acknowledged. From the early Middle Ages onwards, contracts along these lines featured prominently in the aristocratic life of the West. In their specifically feudal form, the lesser man did homage to the greater and received the use of a fixed extent of land in return for performing a fixed roster of military duties. As time passed, arrangements became more flexible, and – as in the Wildenburg case – money played an increasing role. Loyalty and friendship were regularly pledged. But what, in this connection, did 'friendship' entail? Certainly not the intense personal *rapport* of much modern usage: nor the more spiritual, but equally private relationship – 'sharing the counsels of one's heart' – invoked by Saint Augustine and the writers of antiquity. Yet the potency of the term was undoubted. The oldest Germanic texts described as 'battle-friends' those warriors who stood shoulder to shoulder in the face of the enemy. Down the centuries, innumerable legal documents record the role of 'friends and relatives' as advisors in important family transactions. The juxtaposition of the two terms is significant. There may, indeed, be a degree of blurring or overlap between them; the ancient Teutonic root of 'friend' could on occasion be taken to mean 'kinsman'. When Wildenburg used the term in his contract with the Count of Flanders, something of this relationship was suggested. He was henceforth part of that great aristocratic family of which the Count was head; and the future dealings of the two men would proceed on that basis. Some texts make the point particularly explicit. In 1491 the Scottish Earls of Bothwell and Huntly made a bond of friendship. This was very much a pact between social equals, but the mechanism was otherwise similar to the Flemish agreement of 1368. The Earls undertook to be 'tender, kind and loyal' in all their mutual business: just, they added, as fathers, sons, and brothers ought to be. 'Kindness' was after all the proper character of relations between kinsmen.

In dealings between nobles – as equals, or as senior and junior partners – the language of family relations thus extended beyond the ties of blood. This is hardly surprising. The family stood at the heart of aristocratic assumptions about status, wealth and authority; it naturally provided both model and terminology for relationships in the community as a whole. The complexities of the issue should not be underestimated. In the long run, as we shall see, the 'familial' character of dealings between those who held power would largely disappear. And even when attachment to 'kin' and 'friends' was at its most potent, there was ample scope for uncertain or divided loyalty. Were all blood ties of equal force? And could one be 'friend' to more than one lord? There may indeed be some doubt about the character of the family relationship itself. To judge from some recent work on the subject, the aristocratic household of the past offered little scope for warmth or affection: these – like the pursuit of domestic happiness itself – are allegedly the middle-class product of the eighteenth and nineteenth centuries. Whatever the flaws in this argument (nobles of an earlier period may simply have left us less *evidence* of their emotional life), there is no doubt that the aristocratic family could weigh heavily on the individuals who composed it. As we have seen, it was the interests of the collective lineage which shaped the arrangement of marriages and the transmission of property over the generations. But this was the whole point. The family – foundation and embodiment of aristocratic authority – had to take precedence. As in the poorer countries of the modern world, it was the family which offered its members opportunities for help or protection or advancement. These are hardly the priorities of Victorian domesticity. But it would be a mistake to underrate the supportive and protective role of the family in communities without insurance and welfare systems. Support and protection were what kinsmen provided for one another; likewise nobles and their 'friends'.

Whether such relationships involved sentiment and affection is a matter for debate. What is clear is that they were highly valued, and that they shaped the character of aristocratic authority as a whole. The chivalrous orders which played so prominent a role in the noble culture of the late Middle Ages illustrate the point in a number of ways. Edward III's foundation of the Garter and Philip of Burgundy's Golden Fleece gathered great men in a particularly intimate fellowship around their ruler. The knights formed a brotherhood; as brothers they ate together in the ceremonial of banquets, and said fraternal prayers for dead colleagues. Elias Ashmole, the Garter's seventeenth-century chronicler, said that two bonds were the strength of the order: honour and friendship. Honour, as we have seen, implied high birth; and friendship was an extension of the solidarity of kinship. For the noble brothers of the Garter or the Golden Fleece, the family represented the most vivid image of human association in general. Much the same was probably true of Edmund Burke, when in 1790 he described the political community in terms of family affections and the descent of property over the years. Great noble dynasties enjoyed power, prestige and sheer visibility. So it is hardly surprising that the language of leadership and the language of family remained intermingled down the centuries. It was his family which entitled a nobleman (like a king) to wield authority over others; and it was in his family relationships – ranging outward to include 'brothers', friends and others not of his blood – that the core of his power was located. But if this was an essential aspect of the character of aristocratic rule, there is more to be said about what that authority meant in practice.

From the earliest feudal times, moralists had insisted that lordship must be good. Vassals and other subordinates gave their lord obedience and performed such services as custom prescribed. But the relationship was not unconditional. The lord, too, had duties: positively to give physical protection to his men in time of need, and negatively to avoid molesting them in their established rights. An exchange was taking place. And from the sparse records of the barbarian West down to the end of the Middle Ages and beyond, that element of exchange was to play a central role in the contracts and engagements undertaken by nobles: whether with magnates of comparable rank, with lesser men, or indeed with individuals or communities outside the ranks of the privileged altogether. Take, for example, the letter which the Duke of La Force wrote to his tenants in south-west France on inheriting his title in 1713. Lords were placed in authority over others only so as to protect them from oppression, he said: so his father, the late duke, had taught him. 'You will pass on to your children the devotion which you have always had for my house, and I will instil in my heirs the friendship they must show to you . . . as if to their own sons.' The hereditary and 'familial' character of the Duke's authority could hardly have been made more explicit. Mutual ties of affection and support bound together parents and children: so it must be in the larger

seigneurial family. The duke's resounding phrases are a comparatively late, and in their way revealing, restatement of an old ideal.
In the eighteenth century as in the earliest feudal agreements,
lords had duties. But for all its rhetorical flourish, was La Force's
letter anything more than a declaration of principle? The actual
course of relations between nobles and their humblest dependants
often suggested acrimony and violence, not friendship and
devotion. Rent-strikes, litigation, assaults on seigneurial agents:
these were familiar features of the European countryside down
the centuries. Episodic disorder flared intermittently into full-
scale revolt. There will be much to say on this in due course.
Clearly enough, mutual obligations lapsed, sometimes spectacu-
larly so. But this is not to say that they were merely, and at all
times an empty pretence. And the exercise of aristocratic
authority might not necessarily work to the disadvantage of those
who were subject to it.

As La Force said, a principal aristocratic duty was the
protection of one's dependants. This was not wholly myth. Far
back in the Middle Ages, chronic insecurity − invasion by
Magyars or Vikings, fragile government institutions − had made
the search for an armed protector a matter of urgency. By the
process of 'commendation', people of all ranks undertook specific
obligations of service or labour in return for the protection of a
local magnate. This was the logic behind the gradual extensions of
noble power over a hitherto free peasantry. (In one district near
Salzburg, more than 200 independent properties had disappeared
by the year 800, absorbed into the estates of local nobles and of
the Duke of Bavaria.) The castles which were coming to dominate
so much of the European landscape certainly embodied an
increasingly harsh aristocratic 'lordship'. But times were no less
harsh. And the power of the castellans offered at least the
possibility of defence against aggression from outside. In later
periods the nature of the external challenge would undergo a
number of changes. But again, aristocratic leadership might offer
some scope for the defence of the local inhabitants. By the
seventeenth century, central governments throughout Western
Europe were increasingly effective in extracting taxes from their
subjects in the incessant pursuit of military success. Noble
landowners regularly attempted to lessen the burden of their own
tenants. This was not wholly − if at all − a matter of seigneurial

paternalism: more cash paid in tax meant less paid in rent. But the issue provided an undoubted common interest between great man and tenantry. Throughout the wars of Richelieu and of Louis XIV, French government agents incessantly deplored the nobility's failure to co-operate in the drive for efficiency. Accusations of full-scale aristocratic rebellion were generally excessive, at least so far as the collection of tax is concerned. But there is ample proof that influential magnates were ready to use all that influence, at court and in the localities, to discredit government agents and to impede their work. The provinces of south-west France, where the lands of the Duke of La Force chiefly lay, had acquired a particularly troublesome reputation among the tax-agents of the crown: not, perhaps, wholly by coincidence. Here was one issue at any rate where a magnate's tenants might benefit from the 'protection' of which the Duke wrote in 1713: from the authority, that is, which he exercised by right of birth.

Individuals, too, could benefit from that power of command. To serve a man of hereditary rank and power was already to catch a little of his reflected distinction. Obscure birth was no necessary impediment. German historians have been much struck by the *ministeriales* who featured so prominently in the aristocratic entourages of the high Middle Ages. The term suggests nothing more precise than 'agent' in a lord's civil or military dealings. As magnate households grew more elaborate, as the 'artificial' family of clients and retainers expanded, so there was ample scope for competent and energetic men to prosper in a lord's employment. 'Let my agent resolve the disagreements and injuries between these villagers' ruled a Rhenish noble shortly before the end of the eleventh century. The agent remains unnamed and unknown. But to resolve quarrels was to do justice: an act heavy with associations of rank and power. Men such as these were of uncertain status. Few would know the meteoric fortune of Markward, born a serf, who rose under Barbarossa to become Governor of Sicily and Duke of Ravenna at the end of the twelfth century. Here, in particularly spectacular form, is an echo of the question of recruitment raised in the first chapter. The immense staying-power of aristocracy was in part due to the capacity of the ruling class to absorb newcomers of more or less modest origins: and to the determination of those newcomers to get in. Recruits came as we have seen from a variety of sources. But not the least important channel was that taken by the *ministeriales*, and by their later equivalents: estate managers, legal experts, political aides. The prosperous peasant-farmers who were administering the Valencian lands of the Borjas early in the seventeenth century had acquired titles of nobility by the century's end.

Such people had the advantage of contact with a great family. They participated – however humble their initial functions – in the household or the entourage which embodied aristocratic power. The higher one's status and one's ambitions, the more essential it became to establish such contacts as a means to further advancement. Down the centuries the magnetic pull of aristocratic patronage has shaped a good deal of the social and political life of Europe. When the Yorkshire gentleman Sir John Reresby mended an old quarrel with the duke of Norfolk in 1677, he reflected on such matters: we should avoid stooping to 'mean' actions to win a great man's friendship, but honourable opportunities for a reconciliation were on no account to be squandered. Isolation was dangerous. To be taken 'under the care' of a grandee provided an important element in the recipe for social and political success. In the middle of the eighteenth century, aristocratic patrons incessantly lobbied that great power-broker, the Duke of Newcastle, on behalf of gentlemen under their 'care' and 'protection'. Medieval patronage operated in a more martial environment than that of Georgian England, but its logic was not essentially different. Lesser men 'commended themselves' to a feudal superior for advancement and security. And when the Anglo-Saxon author of *The Battle of Maldon* described the horror and shame of flight from the battlefield, he drew a striking picture of the deserter: 'lordless, leaderless, alone . . .'

Order and disorder

The age of the self-made man, clearly, was slow in coming. Connection and patronage were crucial. And it was in the entourage of the great man – radiating out from close kin to professional agents, 'friends' and clients – that they were principally to be found. Centred on the family, hereditary aristocratic leadership found a natural extension in the following or the clientele. Historians have sometimes called these by harsher names. From the French revolution onwards, aristocratic influence came to appear unnacceptable, even openly corrupt. The patron–client relationship was to have no place – or no openly acknowledged one – in the modern political community: least of all a relationship in which the patron's power derived from privileged birth. Aristocratic leadership, in the sense in which this chapter has discussed it, has in due course passed away. This is no doubt as it should be. But it may be unhelpful to regard aristocratic patronage, throughout its centuries-long hey-day, as a wholly negative force. As we have seen, it provided a degree of opportunity for newcomers to gravitate towards power and influence. Before competitive examinations were thought of in the West, before the elaboration of 'scientific' systems of recruitment and personnel management, patronage provided a means – perhaps *the* means – of matching candidates and vacancies. Noble patrons were not necessarily indifferent to the competence of those whose careers they advanced. Macaulay complained to his sister in 1833 of embarrassment at speaking on a cousin's behalf: 'the lad is such a fool that he would utterly disgrace my recommendation.' The tone is distinctively Macaulay's own – effortless and outraged superiority – but no patron felt his cause advanced by association with a manifestly dim protégé. The operation of aristocratic leadership was by definition an inegalitarian business. This is not to say that in a particular historical context it lacked either function or logic.

In a remoter past, the charges against the hereditary power of aristocratic command might appear graver still. The kin, the entourage, the clientele, all offend modern notions of equity and individual rights. In the Middle Ages, in the sixteenth or seventeenth centuries, they could seem to embody anarchy as well. This was what James VI of Scotland had in mind when he wrote of rival entourages 'banging it out bravely', kindred against kindred, to the destruction of crown and commonwealth. Modern historians have been ready in the main to follow the royal cue. So much historical attention has been directed to the study of 'public institutions' – monarchies, parliaments, nation-states – that the distinctive forms of aristocratic power have inevitably appeared both elusive and sinister. Clienteles and entourages suggested faction and violence. In the Wars of the Roses, or in the

Burgundian — Orleanist vendettas of late medieval France, noble
kindreds were indeed at the core of rival parties, and their
antagonism in both cases threatened to engulf the entire
community. In 1464 the great Estremaduran families of Solis and
Monroy exchanged insults at a wedding feast, and their respective
followers found themselves caught up for years in a bush-fire of
violence which swept the whole of southern Spain. Yet here too
context is vital. That aristocratic followings were on occasion
drawn into violence is not in doubt. But the claim that they were
intrinsically violent is another matter. It is not self-evident that
great noblemen, their kinsmen and their clients had much to gain
from participating in indiscriminate civil mayhem. And it may be
significant that each of the famous feuds just mentioned occurred
against a background of markedly incompetent and unpopular
royal government. Energetic rulers offered the hope that conflicts
could be resolved in peaceable trade-offs: and that great men and
their followers could avoid the hazards of 'the way of violence'.

There is a further, and more positive, point to be made. In
periods when the formal mechanisms of the law were slow moving
and inadequate, great men could use their authority to resolve
disputes among their followers. In 1578 a group of Scottish
notables — the Earls of Eglinton and Glencairn, and a number of
prominent lairds — signed an agreement of this kind. Quarrels
had recently erupted among their kinsmen, 'tending to the break
and trouble of the country'; all concerned now agreed to live once
again in the 'amity and kindness' that had once bound them; and
if in future this concord were broken, 'as God forbid', it would be
for the present signatories to take action against the trouble-
makers. There was an echo here of a very ancient understanding
of justice: less the pursuit of individual guilt or innocence than
the re-establishment of peace — 'amity and kindness' — in the
community. Aristocratic authority naturally carried great weight
both in making and in enforcing settlements of this sort. In 1458,
a period of intense political activity, Richard of York found time
to order a group of supporters to put aside 'grouchings and
rancours of hert' and pay due compensation to the kinsfolk of a
man they had killed. At the end of the thirteenth century, a
variant on private peace-making of this kind was recorded in the
Asti region of Piedmont. After years of violent feud, two noble
clans agreed not only to resolve their differences, but to adopt a

common surname and place of residence: and henceforth 'to live with one another in indissoluable brotherhood and unity'.

Once again, the family, and its extension into the entourage and the 'connection', appears at the very core of aristocratic authority. Kinsmen and dependants looked to their patron for leadership, protection and the possibility of arbitration in the disputes of the day. Where government was chronically weak, the hereditary power of a great man offered a degree of order: both among the members of the entourage and in their dealings with the community as a whole. Down to more recent times, aristocratic patronage continued to provide an inescapable element in public life. In the middle of the eighteenth century, the duke of Newcastle furthered the interests of his innumerable 'friends' much as a baronial magnate had done centuries before. For all the difference of context, the mechanism was in essence the same. Lesser men sought the aid of those who had been born to rule. The process is hardly compatible with modern views of public life; but over the centuries this was how aristocratic leadership worked.

Two concluding, and modifying, remarks are relevant. Aristocratic authority derived from birth, and was embodied above all in the family and its 'artificial' counterpart of clientele of entourage. This explains a good deal, but not everything. In some non-European communities, anthropologists have glimpsed what they call a 'kinship polity'. Among Australian aboriginals, or the Tallensi of the Volta, it is claimed that individuals take their identity wholly from the real or adoptive family to which they belong; no distinct public institutions exist. The aristocratic lineages of Europe never monopolized behaviour and attitudes to this extent. A great man's entourage regularly included members whose attachment was at best conditional. Patrons were to an extent dependent on their followers. The Duchess of Norfolk told the Paston family in 1455 that her husband expected loyalty from them and other 'such persons as belong unto him'; but substantial East Anglian gentry were no man's property, not even a duke's, and in later years the Pastons were to move away from their allegiance to the Norfolks. Material calculation made the solidity of the noble entourage uncertain. So did questions of policy and principle. Sir Lewis Namier wrote his great studies of Hanoverian politics largely in terms of aristocratic clienteles and the machinations within and between them. Some expert opinion has cast doubt on the adequacy of such an approach, even for that hard-headed and undogmatic world. Where religious or ideological commitments counted for more, where weighty matters of policy were to be resolved, the potency of aristocratic connection was correspondingly reduced. When noblemen confronted the 'bar-barian' invasion of Italy in 1494, or the religious upheavals in France a hundred years on, or the approach of civil war in seventeenth-century England, ties of family and connection no doubt weighed in their calculations, as they always did. But to analyse their response to great events wholly in these terms is unlikely to prove completely satisfactory.

There is a second point. As we have seen, the family and the entourage provided a means of protection for its members, and a framework for resolving disputes both within the clientele and in the community at large. When public law-enforcement was weak, or lacking, aristocratic leadership might limit the damage. Even feud and vendetta were perhaps less destructive, less purely anarchic, than the outrage of contemporaries might suggest. In the alleged turbulence of fifteenth-century England, a recent student has seen the aristocratic recourse to violence as limited and exceptional. Great men and their followers pursued their interests in the main through a judicious mixture of lawsuits, informal settlements and political lobbying: 'an integral system of social controls, responsive to local and individual needs'. Aristocratic influence is not to be associated with mere disorder, and to that extent the verdict is an illuminating one. But the language of 'systems' and 'controls' raises problems of its own. A central-heating engineer understands the precise interaction of valve and pump and thermostat; the historian's grasp of social structures in the past is of a different order. More concretely, such language fails to address the problem of change. This may have been the way in which nobles exercised their leadership in the fifteenth century, but over time attitudes and behaviour took other forms. The immense potency of hereditary authority remained, as did the significance of family and patronage. Standards and expectations altered nevertheless, and too much reference to 'integral systems of social control' makes it hard to understand why this should have been so. Habits of casual violence, for example, became increasingly unacceptable, both to the public at large and within the privileged class itself. But one change above all was to confront the distinctive hereditary power of aristocracy. This was the increasingly intrusive public authority of the state; and the character of that confrontation will be the subject of the following chapter.

4

Aristocracy and the State

Far back into the Middle Ages, the governments of Europe were extending their powers. Hereditary monarchs, or the ruling councils of free republics such as Florence and Venice, claimed supreme and distinctive authority. In the vernacular languages of the West, one word above all others came to connote that authority: the state. The term was potent, perhaps ominous; and experts remain at odds about a good deal of its history. Was 'state' simply a synonym for 'ruler'? Or was it emerging as a force quite distinct from the person of the prince? And if so, when? These issues need not detain us here. What is clear is that over the centuries government was coming to play an increasingly commanding role at the centre of public life. In 1651 Thomas Hobbes wrote of it as 'that mortal God, to which we owe under the immortal God our peace and defence'. How would aristocratic power come to terms with the demands of that mortal God, the state?

In Weber's language, aristocratic power was traditional, and state power bureaucratic. Nobles commanded others because their families customarily did so; state power meant policy objectives clearly defined − Hobbes's 'peace and defence' − and efficiently pursued. Professor Stone has argued that a 'natural enmity' existed between the two. The state's demand for obedience inevitably cut across the various forms of aristocratic leadership − kinship, clientage, local influence − discussed in the previous chapter. Conflict was certainly possible. In England such measures as the Statute of 1390 attempted to limit the numbers of armed retainers who took service with a great lord. In the city-republics of the Mediterranean, fourteenth- and fifteenth-century legislation disbarred patrician fathers, sons, and brothers from serving together on the same governing councils. (And in

Venice a regulation of 1505 was to restrict the right of noblemen to stand as godfathers: private aristocratic connections might damage the public interest.) By the later Middle Ages, institutions like the English College of Heralds or the Spanish 'Judges of the Nobility' placed the scrutiny of claims to noble status squarely in the hands of royal officials. Government regulation of aristocratic affairs was on the increase, and sometimes more than regulation. Already in the twelfth century, English chroniclers were observing that kings habitually used 'sheer arbitary force' (*vis et voluntas*) to deprive great men of their lands, or worse. A Catalan jurist, Tomas Mieres, wrote in the 1440s that kings had a duty to ignore baronial jurisdiction when tenants were suffering ill-treatment: necessity – defined by the crown and its agents – eclipsed hereditary rights. Mieres's royal master, Alfonso 'the Magnanimous', King of Aragon and Naples, no doubt had the principle in mind during these years as he set about placing noble franchises in his Italian lands under the direct control of the crown. Public authority claimed a power of regulation over the activities of those born to high rank. And positive action on occasion followed.

By the sixteenth and seventeenth centuries, 'positive action' was becoming more frequent, and more contentious. This may in part reflect changing perceptions among the agents of government. It has been argued that officials and publicists during this period were attempting to impose more rigorous standards of public order; aristocratic conduct which failed to conform was defined as subversive, and repressed accordingly. By an edict of 1626 the French government attempted to outlaw the current noble craze of duelling. Two well-connected counts, Bouteville and des Chapelles, challenged the ban by staging their celebrated public bout in the middle of Paris. Arrest, trial, and condemnation to death promptly followed. Friends and kinspeople of the two men petitioned Louis XIII and his chief minister, Richelieu, in the name of clemency and honour. But this was just the point. Two gentlemen of rank had placed their innate honour – their right to duel – above the authority of the state. Only one outcome was possible, and the two men duly died: by the sword, as their status required. There was no doubt an element of the symbolic in all this. But in an age of limited literacy, symbols had their own impact on opinion. The spectacle of trial and execution gave physical expression to the supremacy of state power over the individual, no matter how exalted his rank. Or as Richelieu put it during the affair of the duel, honour must everywhere take precedence – *except* when the interest of the state was at issue.

The day-to-day necessities of government created further possibilities of friction between state and aristocracy. The colossal growth in military and naval expenditure between 1500 and 1700 meant a corresponding drive to increase revenues. In the aftermath of the Reformation, both Catholic and Protestant states sought to maintain and increase control over the religious life of their respective peoples. This meant increased government intervention. Nobles found their tenants subject to unprecedented demands for tax, their own privileges at risk, and their hereditary leadership of the local community threatened by interference from outside. State power could come to confront aristocratic power. On occasion, the result was open conflict. When Philip II of Spain was attempting to tighten administrative control over his Netherlands possessions early in the 1560s, it was the magnates of the region – Egmont, Aerschot – who led the first stages of resistance to his plans. When Catalonia was on the verge of rebellion against Spain's financial demands in 1639, it was a member of one of the oldest families of the region, Diego de Rocaberti, who travelled to the capital with a list of aristocratic grievances against Madrid's arrogance. And when the Scots drew up their National Covenant in 1638 – in protest against the new religious programme imposed on them by the Stuart government in London – it was such Lowland noblemen as Rothes, Balmerino and Montrose who took a leading part in the movement.

A collision course was thus sometimes hard to avoid. Governments had their own urgent priorities – fighting wars, maintaining religious control – and in pursuing them they imposed a harsh burden on the community. When the community erupted in protest, aristocracy provided leadership that was (in the most literal sense) 'natural': a hereditary, customary authority over others. And this might on occasion involve leadership of the community against the power of the state. But 'might' is the correct, strictly conditional, word. The consequences of rebellion could prove as unattractive to nobles as the pressures which provoked it. The three cases just cited make the point with particular force. In each, events moved quickly beyond the control of the original aristocratic leaders. Both in the Netherlands and in Scotland, power passed increasingly into the hands of militant Protestants, both preachers and lay activists. After 1640 a movement for total separation from Spain began to get under way in Catalonia, led in the main by small-town politicians. Zealots for religion, or for national independence, were notoriously indifferent to the age-old claims of aristocratic leadership: blue blood or not, loyalty to the cause was the thing. Noblemen generally took the point. Worse tyrannies might threaten their position than the occasional excesses of the state. In the Netherlands the great landowners of Brabant and Hainault gradually drifted back into allegiance to the Spanish crown. The Catalan aristocracy showed little desire to follow their more nationalist (and humbly-born) compatriots. After the troubles of the mid-seventeenth century, relations between the Spanish crown and its greater subjects became tolerable once more. Spain was certainly a great monarchy, thought an English diplomat in 1691, 'yet it has at present much aristocracy in it.' And when order returned to Scotland in 1660, it was through great nobles like Lauderdale and Rothes that the new king (Charles II) governed his northern lands. They were friends and relatives of those who had led opposition to the 'Stuart tyranny' in 1638. But the intervening years had shown where rebellion could lead. Disorder and religious conflict left no nobleman safe. The Marquis of Montrose had been a hero of national resistance in the early years of the troubles: in 1650 a tribunal of hard-line Protestants judged that he had betrayed the cause of the godly, and condemned him to a plebeian death by hanging. For noblemen, the moral could hardly be more plain.

The logic of compromise

At its most interventionist, the state might goad noblemen into resistance. But *even* at its most interventionist, the state was likely to appear less alarming than the social upheavals which resistance was all too liable to bring in its wake. This explains a good deal about the limits to aristocratic rebellion. It also suggests a cogent practical reason for government and noblemen attempting, so far as possible, to avoid open conflict. Compromise, for a variety of causes, made sense.

This was the more true because for much of the European past states enjoyed little direct power to govern the territories over which they claimed sovereignty. Poor communications hampered any rapid response to local problems; and, together with a perennial shortage of cash, they long impeded the development of a reliable local bureaucracy. So the agents of the state had to come to terms.

From early medieval times on, power in the localities was essentially aristocratic: hereditary control which certain families exercised over land and people. If the authority of the state was to have any reality, this was in turn the reality with which it had to work. A great historian, F. W. Maitland, described the administration of England in the Middle Ages as 'self-government at the king's command'. The king's command was a mark of his royal sovereignty. But its enforcement was dependent on the co-operation of the 'natural' leaders of the local community, shire-knights and territorial magnates. No medieval sovereign could ignore the power of the Marcher lords to impose a rough order in the Welsh borderlands, nor that of Cliffords or Percies in the north.

Over time, of course, the balance of these relationships slowly shifted. The resources of central government grew, which meant that the state could become more demanding and selective in its choice of local power-brokers. Some historians have argued that a decisive change occurred when rulers felt sufficient confidence to appoint 'outsiders' as important regional agents. It may be significant that under the strong rule of Elizabeth, two strangers to the north of England, Sussex and Huntingdon, held office as Lord President in the royal council at York. Outsiders or not, however, both men were indisputably aristocrats. And for as long as aristocracy existed, the state stood to benefit from a careful harnessing of the authority which it exercised. After lengthy debate in 1634, the Spanish government appointed the young and inexperienced Constable of Castile to military command on the Basque frontier; the decision went in his favour because of the influence in the region which his family had traditionally enjoyed. In the eighteenth century, the kingdom of Prussia struck contemporary opinion as a marvel of bureaucratic efficiency, but here too aristocratic influence played its part. The essential agent of local government – the *Landrat* – was regularly selected from the land- (and serf-) owning nobility of the province in which he was to work.

So if state power and aristocratic power met in occasional noisy collisions, conflict was by no means inevitable. Far from it. Great men wielded authority over kin, clients, and often much of their local community too. With such men, governments had everything to gain from co-operation: and from ensuring that they had sufficient influence to 'deliver' their entourage as well. In a more remote past this was the logic behind such texts as the constitution on feudal rights issued by the Emperor Barbarossa in 1158. This insisted on the aristocratic duty of service to the Emperor as sovereign. But it also documented and clarified the powers which nobles wielded over lesser men; it was their standing as lords, as natural leaders, which after all made them valuable allies of the Emperor in the first place. In a very different context, a similar logic was at work in the agreement which agents of the Scottish crown signed with a number of Hebridean chieftains at Iona in 1609. The purpose of the meeting was to subject the inhabitants of the Western Isles to the discipline of the Reformed Kirk. The government was also attempting to end what it saw as the endemic disorderliness of the Hebridean people, caused, among other things, 'by their extraordinary drinking of strong wines and aquavit'. But how, in such wild parts, could the crown achieve these admirable objectives? Once more the policy of the state had to be mediated through the great men of the region and their followers. It was they who signed the agreement: Hector Maclean of Duart, Donald Gorm Macdonald of Sleat, Rory Macleod of Harris, 'together with the most part of their friends, followers and tenants'. Each leader was to be answerable for his men, and was empowered to bring any breaker of the agreement before the king's justice. Lordship in all its senses was a reality with which the state had to reckon. Shrewdly handled, it could provide a resource for the state to exploit.

In its own way, too, the state provided a resource for noblemen: another inducement toward compromise rather than conflict. In 1609 the Macleans and Macdonalds no doubt anticipated future royal favours in return for their readiness to co-operate with the king's agents. Far from working towards its inevitable destruction, government activity might provide aristocratic influence with the means to thrive. Earlier chapters have already touched on the point in a number of ways. Crown service, civil or military, was a route to enhanced status: from solid gentility as a Cecil or a Wellesley to titled distinction as Salisbury or Wellington. As Gilbert de Lannoy had pointed out in the fifteenth century, service to the ruler was also a properly aristocratic means of acquiring wealth. The career of the Cecils or a Wellington certainly made that point clearly enough; and government favours could ease hard-pressed noble fortunes in less spectacular fashion too, by the grant of a pension or of permission to sell off an entailed estate. And as the educational standards which public service demanded rose, so the state continued to provide opportunities for those nobles alert enough to adapt. The intensely aristocratic character of the Victorian foreign office, or of the Prussian bureaucracy during the same period, suggests the continuing success of that adaptation.

A vocation for gentlemen

The state, down to a very recent past, was a source of aristocratic opportunity. But in important respects the connection went deeper than that. Birth, after all, conferred authority, whether that authority was exercised in the local rule of a medieval castellan or the parliamentary following of a Hanoverian grandee. And it was natural enough that noblemen should gravitate towards power in its most visible form: government itself. This was a part of the aristocratic condition, and it was as true in nineteenth-century England as in the entourage of a medieval king. The chronicler Orderic Vitalis noted that in 1066 the Conqueror made good use of the advice of his counsellors, and of the courage 'which they had inherited from their ancestors'. Eight centuries on, these aristocratic virtues would perhaps have meant something to Lord Salisbury when he formed his third Cabinet, in 1895; commoners, as in his previous administrations, would be in a clear minority among his new colleagues. A distinguished ancestry obliged men to serve the state: this was the view of a provincial magistrate writing to the chancellor of France in 1602. The point was a commonplace down the centuries. And it carried a more menacing corollary. If those born to it lacked the wit or training to govern, 'meaner men's sons' would take over. The phrase comes from the Tudor educationist Roger Ascham, and it too was something of a commonplace over the years. To fulfil their public role, nobles had to adapt as cultural and educational standards changed. That public role, after all, was at the centre of Ascham's argument. Unless sheer incompetence opened the way to their social inferiors, nobles were natural leaders in the expanding business of the state.

As illustration, take the agreement drawn up by a group of English magnates in 1308. This was early in the reign of Edward II. Political tensions were growing. The signatories of the text – the Earls of Lincoln, Pembroke and others – warned Edward of mounting royal unpopularity. As great men of the realm, the Earls owed the king their allegiance, and so – as they explained – had a duty to speak out against actions in his name which threatened to undermine his honour. This was another expression of the traditional emphasis on 'counsel', already met with. Lords had a right to ask for advice: followers a duty to provide it, palatable or otherwise. At the level of kings and magnates, the giving of counsel necessarily impinged on matters of state. Their birth destined men such as Pembroke and Lincoln to political activity, and political leadership.

Some historians have seen in actions of this sort a kind of 'aristocratic constitutionalism'. Three generations before the text of 1308 was drafted, the representatives of the English nobility gave King John the benefit of their advice, and the result was indeed one of the more celebrated constitutional documents of Western history. In Magna Carta, the early clauses dealt specifically with the rights of those who held their lands direct from the crown, men such as the aristocratic signatories of the text themselves. But it was unmistakeably a document of state as well, with its attention to the proper processes of the law, to policy towards Wales and Scotland, and to the future running of the kingdom as a whole. The great men at Runnymede – Arundel and Salisbury, assorted Bassetts and Fitzherberts – inherited the power and the duty to bring an erratic king to heel. And something of the kind was involved in a number of later scuffles between governments and nobles, as we have already glimpsed. The grievances of the Catalans or the Netherlanders against the government in Madrid, the uproar provoked in Scotland by the policies of Charles I: all these were matters of the most urgent public protest. In crises such as these, the natural leaders of the community had an equally natural, and equally aristocratic, role in pointing up the acceptable limits to the power of the state.

Whether this role is best described as 'constitutional' may be open to question. The term implies attachment to a precise body of rules, written or not; and it may conjure up unhelpful notions of a clear-cut distinction between government and opposition. It is hard to know what 'constitution' could have meant in such authoritarian regimes as those of seventeenth-century France or eighteenth-century Prussia. And it is a central argument of this chapter that the activities of governments and nobles were so enmeshed for so much of the European past that any concept of permanent aristocratic opposition is unlikely to make much sense. What was clearly at issue was an inherited vocation for leadership in public affairs. Where the initiatives of the state appeared arbitrary or otherwise oppressive, this vocation might lead to occasional cautious and temporary bouts of resistance. More typically, aristocratic assumptions seemed to encourage noblemen towards co-operation with, and participation in, the business of government. A representative of the nobility at the French Estates-General of 1588 told his audience that he represented not merely the nobles of his own day, but all the aristocratic generations that had gone before: it was the ancestral example of 'inherited generosity' that inspired their successors to serve the state. The rhetoric would have done credit to Burke himself. The sentiment was certainly tenacious. In 1784 the Venetian nobleman Andrea Tron returned to the connection between aristocratic ancestry and leadership in state affairs. Addressing the senate, he recalled that a patrician's upbringing had taught him the public responsibilities of high birth: and went on to urge the Republic to undertake economic modernization along northern European lines as a matter of social and political urgency. Andrea died the following year, but an echo of his attitudes can be caught in the will drawn up by his kinsman Francesco Tron in 1793. Francesco had no sons but two daughters. He accordingly instructed his executors to arrange that they each marry young patricians of limited means and good character; the young men were then to devote their share of the Tron inheritance to the pursuit of careers in public life. Only four years later, the armies of the French revolution would reach

Venice, and sweep away its aristocratic institutions for ever. But the will of Francesco Tron makes as clear as any literary text the continuing force of the connection between aristocratic birth and a commitment to public life.

Gentlemen were destined for public affairs, for participation in the activities of the state. It was natural to assume that the converse held good as well: that public affairs were essentially a matter for the well-born. The career of Cardinal Richelieu is a case in point. He was no friend to what he chose to define as aristocratic disorder; it was in those terms that he confronted the craze for duelling, as we have seen, and he suppressed it with corresponding ruthlessness. The public authority of the state must come first. But it is unlikely that Richelieu saw any fundamental conflict between the interests of monarchy and aristocracy. It was rather a matter of persuading noblemen to direct their thirst for honour toward the service of the crown: hardly a surprising outlook on the part of the cardinal and minister whose own ancestry reached back (allegedly) as far as the Crusaders. Even Thomas Hobbes referred at times to the distinctive role taken within the community by those whom he called 'generous natures'. Hobbes's view of the character and powers of the state − that mortal God − could scarcely have been more authoritarian. But the language of 'generosity' and 'nature' suggested a continuing association between aristocracy and political leadership. Leviathan might be sovereign, but gentlemen − the *generosi*, the well-born − would give the orders.

Over the centuries, theorists and agents of governments were undoubtedly working towards a more rigorous and demanding view of the state. In the very long run, as we shall see, it would also become possible to conceive the relationship between state and citizen as one in which inherited rank and status would play no part. But the process was slow and uncertain. Thinking about power remained muffled, permeated by the sense that some were born to it and others not. The hierarchy of birth and privilege formed part of the natural order of things. No state could subsist by detaching itself from the order which that hierarchy represented, still less by challenging it. Late in the eighteenth century, for instance, Carl Friedrich of Baden earned a justified European reputation for energetic and enlightened rule. The full authority of his little state was brought to bear for the protection of religious minorities: and for reforming the more scandalous injustices suffered by peasant communities. Yet the suggestion that aristocratic privilege was in itself unjust struck him as scandalous, a certain recipe for the overthrow of the state. More than that, hierarchy was *natural* (Carl Friedrich pointed to the analogous 'animal kingdom'), so the denial of its place in public life amounted, quite literally, to absurdity. This was very much the note which Carl's contemporary Louis XVI struck in his celebrated proclamation of June 1789. With government at a standstill and an assortment of pressure groups lobbying for more or less radical measures of reform, the king issued a resounding commitment to uphold the inherited privileges of the French nobility. The intimate bonding between noblemen and monarchy could have been taken for granted at most periods over the preceding thousand years. By 1789 some contemporaries were beginning to call that relationship into question. But anachronism or not, the royal declaration meant that the Bourbon flagship sailed into the maelstrom of revolution flying the banner of aristocracy alongside the fleur-de-lis.

Over the centuries, it was thus hard to conceive of the activities of the state without reference to the aristocratic personnel on whom the public authorities so largely relied: or to the equally aristocratic assumptions which that personnel brought to their work. Public life was indisputably the business of gentlemen. Its style and character were shaped accordingly. Indeed 'public' may be the wrong term. When aristocracy held sway, politics easily took on the appearance of a private pastime for contending lineages and their hangers-on: an extension, that is, of the forms of connection discussed in the preceding chapter. Early in the reign of Ferdinand and Isabella (in 1476), the Spanish government decided to pardon the Castilian family of Chaves for its alleged involvement in the political disorders of recent years. This meant that not merely immediate kinsfolk, but a whole range of clients, servants and dependants were able to participate in political activity once again: 193 men in all. Success in public life was in large part a matter of steering one's way through noble followings of this kind. In early fourteenth-century England, Robert Holland was an inconspicuous Lancashire gentlemen when he became associated with the greatest magnate of the day, Thomas of Lancaster. Holland rose to become Lancaster's principal counsellor, and he acquired a substantial fortune along the way: as well as a nasty reputation in his native county for extortion and intermittent violence. In 1322 Lancaster's career ended in military defeat and subsequent execution. But Holland deserted his master at the right moment, and escaped the wreck; two generations on, his heirs would rank as earls and dukes in the entourage of Richard II.

As time wore on, the penalties for political failure became less bloody. But the character of political relationships remained in many respects strikingly similar. Aristocratic connection – or 'neighbourhood, friendship and relation', as Lord Chandos put it to the Tory leader Robert Harley in 1695 – lost none of its significance in public life. Successful politicians were expected to provide appropriate benefits for 'neighbours, friends and relatives', and it was to such personal followings that great men looked for their political support. At the beginning of the reign of George III, the parliamentary politics of Wiltshire took on a positively baronial flavour: the Duke of Marlborough offered potential voters hunting rights in his forest of Savernake, while Lord Bruce wooed them with the prospect of gargantuan venison suppers. Entertainment of this kind certainly succeeded on occasion in winning new 'friends' for noble patrons. In 1756, the Earl of Uxbridge surprised a local magistrate by the despatch of a suitably aristocratic gift – a doe from his Staffordshire estates. The magistrate's letter of acknowledgement was appropriately fulsome: and it ended with the assurance that 'should I ever be honoured in any commands for your lordship's service, they shall with great pleasure punctually be obeyed . . .'

The private relationship of the aristocratic entourage thus shaped – even if they did not wholly determine – the workings of politics. The bonds of leadership and service which drew together lesser and greater men extended into the wider world of politics. This was true of the pursuit of local influence, as Uxbridge's cultivation of a potential county supporter suggests. But it held equally good for kings and princes at the centre of the political world: and for those who looked to them for advancement. In an important sense, rulers were the leaders of the greatest of all aristocratic entourages. And like those of other lords, their followers were bound to them by personal obligations of honour and service.

In medieval times, these relations were often expressed in explicitly feudal terms. At Salisbury in 1086, the greater land-owners of England swore allegiance to the king — the conqueror — from whom, directly or indirectly, their estates were held. In a rather later period, kings and princes used the bonds of chivalry — the 'brotherhood' or 'fellowship' of the nobly-born — to draw important followers around them. Comradeship shaded into politics. (When the Duke of Burgundy moved into a particularly cautious diplomatic agreement with England in 1419, he avoided membership of the Order of the Garter.) Nowhere was the king more clearly a noble patron writ large than in the functioning of the court. Here was the apogee of lordly display and 'entertain-ment'. Household officers for Queen Elizabeth — not the most extravagant of monarchs — budgeted for an annual consumption of 40,000 chickens, half a million gallons of beer, and four million eggs. Nor was this *mere* display. The royal court was the grandest expression of the aristocratic entourage, in which deals were struck and great men helped lesser ones toward advancement. During the reign of Edward IV, John Paston wrote to a kinsman that the surest way to further the family's business was to make contact with the courtiers 'who lie nightly in the king's chamber'. The advice was relevant far beyond the context of fifteenth-century England. Part masking it, part symbolizing it, court life centred on the pursuit of power. Families born to rank wielded an authority over their followers that, as we have seen, blended the domestic, the ceremonial, and the political. At the royal court, the first gentleman of the kingdom provided the most glittering example of the style. Historians have sometimes associated the more spectacular courts, and in particular Louis XIV's Versailles, with mindless display, aristocratic decadence, and increasingly total royal control over public life. This is unconvincing. The political prizes to be won at court were real enough; and sensible kings knew the value of keeping in close touch with powerful noblemen and their clienteles. Over the centuries, the resources of central governments unquestionably grew, and the glamour of a Versailles, or a Schönbrunn, or a Buen Retiro, testified to the fact. But the profoundly aristocratic character of court life reflected the state's equally deep-rooted accommodation with noble power, not a disposition to trample it down. In 1675, the French general Turenne fell in battle on the Rhine, and received a hero's burial at Saint-Denis among the tombs of his country's kings. Court gossips struck a less elevated note: the friends of the late viscount feared impending exclusion from influence, while his enemies were all optimism. The Sun King pondered his schemes for European conquest, but aristocratic politics went on.

Vested interests, old and new

Almost a century earlier, the essayist Montaigne had described the French monarchy — then beset by civil war — as 'just, tolerable, and aristocratic'. The first two adjectives may be open to question. But the aristocratic character of the state was undeniable: and not only in France, nor only in the sixteenth and seventeenth centuries. This was true of the personnel who participated in the state's activities; it was true of the assumptions which they brought to their work; and it was true of much of the style of political life in general. Yet Montaigne's remark raises a number of further issues.

However aristocratic its character, the scale of government activity down the centuries was inescapably growing. This was partly a gradual process, the slow imposition of higher standards of public order, and partly a series of erratic reactions to short-term necessity — in particular to the spiralling costs of war. Nobles and commoners alike found frequent occasion to grumble about increasing burdens of taxation and government surveillance. More specifically they grumbled about the alleged beneficiaries of this increased state activity: functionaries, financiers, and a whole range of government contractors. Back in the twelfth century, an Anglo-Norman chronicler was already complaining about the men of obscure origin, 'risen from the dust', who were using their position in the royal service to oppress the community at large. Bureaucratic expansion not only hit the taxpayer's pocket; it offended his social prejudices as well. By the sixteenth and seventeenth centuries, the 'men risen from the dust' had become a stereotype for general abuse: government agents of dubious origin, exploiting public office for their own advantage. In a (too) much quoted phrase, the duke of Saint-Simon called the reign of Louis XIV a regime of 'vile bourgeois', and summed up in two words the grievances of centuries. But the judgement hardly squares with contemporaries' impression, noted a little earlier, of a court gripped by the manoeuvres of rival noble clienteles. Government service certainly provided a route to social advancement for those involved in it: newcomers as well as those of established rank. Yet here too, aristocratic assumptions ran very deep.

For one thing, a successful bureaucratic career was hardly to be contemplated without the active support of a patron. Indeed 'bureaucratic' may carry wholly misleading associations. Regular, impersonal systems of appointment and promotion in the public service are in most Western countries a creation of the nineteenth century. In earlier periods, the ambitious functionary, however gifted, attached himself to the interests of a great man, as client, dependant, or (a favourite word) 'creature'. As late as the reign of George III, senior Treasury officials regularly resigned when their aristocratic masters went out of government. 'Public' administration, like politics in general, appeared for much of the time an extension of the personal connections between patrons and their followers. The career of José Gonzales typified thousands. José was an obscure advocate at the Valladolid bar when (in 1624) he entered the service of the Count-duke of Olivares. Olivares, a leading Castilian grandee, enjoyed effective power as chief minister of Spain; and with this formidable support José embarked on a career which brought him conspicuous personal wealth and – as President of the Council of the Indies – high public office. To explain José's success simply in terms of aristocratic patronage would be to ignore the ability and energy which made him an attractive agent for Olivares in the first place. But no ambitious newcomer to public life could ignore the benefits which a noble patron might provide.

Success in government service also carried aristocratic associations of its own. Some senior offices conferred a kind of *de facto* noble status on those who held them, and many more carried the coveted privilege of immunity from direct taxation. In 'bureauratic' Prussia, the government was extending the range of this exemption for high officials as late as the end of the eighteenth century. And in any case, families which rose to prominence in the service of the state were unlikely to resist the immense – and highly aristocratic – attractions of landownership. Land, as we have seen, was no mere real-estate; its possession implied rank and authority. The countryside around capital cities, or important regional centres of government, bore the mark of new men and their ambitions. Villas outside Barcelona or Naples, the great *château*-vineyards of Bordeaux, country houses in Surrey or the Chilterns: all testified, over generations and centuries, to the determination with which successful functionaries sought to turn themselves and their descendants into gentlemen. In 1541 Francisco de los Cobos, one of the most powerful state secretaries in sixteenth-century Spain, entailed his estates in a *mayorazgo* befitting the great man he had become. Suitably enough, the document included a reminder to his heirs and executors that they remember 'the name, reputation and lineage of los Cobos' and do all in their power to conserve them. True to aristocratic form, the success of an individual (however glittering) was simply one stage in the consolidation of a dynasty.

The grander forms of public service, even undertaken by men of modest origins, thus involved unmistakeable signs of social distinction. The low-born functionary certainly provided a stock target for anger and derision: the butt of noblemen and commoners alike. In reality, state servants − from whatever background − made their way in a world where aristocratic influence and aristocratic attitudes were long inescapable. The most successful of them − like los Cobos − achieved visible aristocratic rank in the form of titles, land and power. Down the centuries the service of government implied not an alternative aristocratic distinction, but a means for newcomers to acquire it: both for themselves and for their heirs. (Montaigne, landowner and royal magistrate, praised the 'aristocratic' character of monarchy. His family had been active in maritime trade only two generations earlier.) Certainly, older grandees could joke or sneer at the expense of *arriviste* pen-pushers. At the higher levels of professional success, the upstart might nevertheless offer resources of influence and wealth which proved hard to ignore. Saint-Simon no doubt regarded Louis XIV's finance-minister Colbert as the epitome of the 'vile bourgeois'. But the three Colbert daughters married dukes. A distinguished servant of the state thus achieved conspicuous social success, and three ducal families acquired conveniently direct access to the centre of power.

The activities of government became more extensive. But gentlemen, of old − and of less old − family continued to exercise leadership as part of their birthright. 'Birthright' is no mere metaphor. A flying start in public life was part of the young nobleman's inheritance. Two critics of the aristocratic influence in the British army noted in 1865 that Welleseley was a general at thirty; however distinguished, commoners like Campbell or Havelock spent half their service careers reaching the same rank. Lord Chesterfield told his son in 1749 that he would have a seat in the Commons as soon as he came of age. The rise of the younger Pitt − Chancellor of the Exchequer at twenty-three − was striking by any standards, but hardly freakish: a young nobleman inherited his public role as surely as he inherited rank itself.

Indeed the offices of state frequently passed permanently into aristocratic hands, and became in the process a kind of private patrimony. Far back in the Middle Ages, such surnames as Stewart or Visconti marked the hereditary prominence of great families in the service − as 'stewards' or 'viscounts' − of king or emperor. As government institutions became more elaborate, 'patrimonial' influence extended correspondingly. In seventeenth-century Spain, candidates for public office compiled 'memorials of nobility' in the hope of attracting royal or ministerial favour; these texts (often highly tendentious) documented the petitioner's illustrious birth, and his family's distinguished record of crown service. Here, as in so much else, the claims of ancestry counted. From time to time, government agents no doubt saw the possibility of conflict between public and private (or family) interest; in most Western countries, legislation attempted to limit the numbers of kinsmen who served together on official business. But political reality imposed its own logic. Wise rulers down the centuries accepted the force of heredity in the administration of the state just as they had to come to terms with it in the life of the community at large. Kings regularly permitted members of favoured families to by-pass statutory regulations against kinship; with royal approval, public office frequently passed − like land or title − from father to son. In 1655 the French government allowed two members of the Le Tellier family, the war minister and his teenage heir, to share the post of state secretary between them; if sons were encouraged to follow the distinguished example of their father, so the letter of privilege explained, the state itself was likely to benefit.

Few governments have had more energetic servants than the

elder and younger Le Tellier; the family fully earned the privilege which the state had granted it in 1655. The juxtaposition of 'family' and 'state' is crucial. Public life down the centuries was profoundly affected by aristocratic assumptions about heredity, rank and power. Great families wielded public authority by right of birth; relative newcomers − like the elder Le Tellier − passed on distinction and responsibility to later generations. Hierarchy was in the most literal sense a part of the natural order. Thinking about the state long took as its point of departure the premise that some were born to command and others to obey. In the middle of the eighteenth century, Montesquieu saw a hereditary nobility as fundamental to the character of monarchical regimes; men born to distinction naturally − he thought − pursued honour in the service of their royal master. Montesquieu came of a long line of landowners and officials. And he summed up, from first-hand experience, a way of thinking about public affairs which had held sway for the better part of a thousand years.

Yet when Montesquieu's views appeared in print (in 1748), some reactions proved hostile. The most strident attack came from Voltaire. He thought it scandalous that mere birth should qualify a handful of men to wield authority over others. As the eighteenth century wore on, such criticisms gathered momentum. Some bold spirits began to challenge the aristocratic link between birth, hierarchy and power. Perhaps men could live in harmony without submitting to the constraints of rank and privilege. And perhaps such constraints infringed the rights of individual men. By 1790 Edmund Burke saw the whole aristocratic order threatened by subversive ideologies. Rank and heredity were at risk, their distinctive claims to authority disregarded, or denied, in the name of democratic equality and the unrestrained power of the state. These and other 'odious maxims' form the subject-matter of the next, and final, chapter. Critics of aristocracy have never been wholly silent. And in the very long run they brought aristocratic power to an end, as Burke feared that they would.

5

Challenge and Retreat

The limits of resistance

In 1793 an anonymous contemporary of Edmund Burke distri-
buted a handbill in the streets of Norwich. The text noted the
recent death of Lord Buckingham, and pointed out that the late
peer 'had thirty thousand pounds yearly for setting his arse in the
House of Lords and doing nothing'. This provides a welcome
contrast to the more unctuous expressions of respect for
aristocratic authority (and for the mother of parliaments). The
view may owe something, in 1793, to the influence of radical
opinions from America or France. But down the long centuries of
aristocratic domination, a number of arguments had provided
material with which to challenge the hereditary authority of the
well-born.

One source of such arguments was (perhaps unexpectedly) the
ancient world. The immense influence of classical antiquity on
the civilization of the West has not, in the main, worked in the
direction of social levelling. The systematic study of Latin and
Greek was always the preserve of a leisured minority. The
political ideas of Plato, or of the Stoics – at any rate as they were
received in the post-classical world – appeared to assume the
existence of a natural elite of rulers. Yet Aristotle had included
'democracy' in his survey of constitutions. And the evidence of
ancient history – perhaps above all the stirring deeds of
republican Rome – survived to remind later generations of what
could be achieved by a community of free men. This historical
model fascinated Machiavelli, whose reputation has been permanently distorted by his authorship of *The Prince*. At the heart
of his concern lay the possibility of (re)creating a body of citizens
with civil rights to exercise and the military force to defend them.
In such a community, the hereditary power of 'gentlemen'
appeared to Machiavelli an inevitably disruptive and corrupting

force. Citizenship, not rank or hierarchy, was to be the bond which held civil society together. The urban politics of Italy provided a particularly fertile environment for criticisms of aristocracy along these lines; the idea of common citizenship was after all probably most easily grasped within the walls of a great city such as Florence. But the idea could be exported. During the upheavals of the English civil wars, a number of radicals looked back to the ancient world for guidance in establishing genuinely republican institutions. In the early 1650s the journal *Mercurius Politicus* was carrying regular warnings against any return to 'kingly' or 'settled' power: to the power, that is, of a hereditary monarch – or of a hereditary aristocracy.

Not only intellectuals invoked the past as a basis for criticism of the (aristocratic) present. Country people regularly claimed that nobles' demands for payments or services breached the traditional usages of earlier times. At the beginning of the tenth century, texts from the region of Lake Como record an early dispute which centred on an issue of this kind: were the labour-services then demanded of tenants the same as those in the Emperor Lothar's day, two generations before? It was in periods of major economic adjustment that landowners were most likely to impose new demands, and anti-aristocratic feeling became correspondingly acute. Fifteenth-century Catalonia was gripped by a bitter rural war between peasants and nobles; a crucial ingredient in the conflict was the attempt by landowners to offset the long-term effects of the Black Death – falling population, falling income from rent – by imposing the hated cash fines called 'evil customs'. And something of the sort may lie behind the German Peasants' War of 1525. Rural manifestos repeatedly attacked 'innovations' by landowners: in the form of increased rents, encroachments on common land, and the extension or reintroduction of serfdom. Some rebels moved from criticism of seigneurial abuses to outright denial of aristocratic lordship itself. In the spring of 1526 the Tirolean leader, Michael Gaismair, drafted a series of ordinances which sounded a particularly radical note: henceforth, all distinctions of rank were to lapse, and equality (*ain ganze Glaichait*) would reign throughout the community.

Rural protests regularly criticized the behaviour of noblemen in the name of long-established custom. Gaismair's programme suggests how drastic the implications of these apparently conservative grievances might sometimes become. And the Tirolean ordinances have a further significance. Gaismair was a radical Protestant in the heyday of the early Reformation, and he based his plans for social reconstruction on an appeal to 'the holy word of God'. Over the centuries, religion was to provide the most potentially devastating weapon for enemies of aristocratic power. Professor Stone has suggested, for example, that the Puritan ethic significantly eroded the prestige of the seventeenth-century English peerage: nobles were to enjoy public respect for as long as they conformed to godly standards, and otherwise not. The issue is complex, and controversial. Puritanism owed a good deal to aristocratic support, after all, and not a few Puritans came of noble stock. Puritan or otherwise, churchmen found the claims of blood hard to avoid; as the first chapter noted, the presumption of aristocratic leadership counted for much, even in matters of religion. But the possibilities of social criticism were there nevertheless. The New Testament cannot easily be read as a celebration of hereditary wealth and power; and in moments of tension it was from scripture − often second-hand, via preachers or pamphleteers − that rebels drew some of their most subversive slogans. In the German troubles of 1525–6, Luther's doctrine of 'Christian freedom' was invoked to justify action against the great landowners. Before the English Peasants' Revolt of 1381, the priest John Ball recalled the primitive equality of Eden, and set that biblical example alongside the arrogance of the contemporary nobility. 'Who was *then* the gentleman?' was a commonplace of medieval sermons: a preacher's warning against aristocratic excess. At moments of crisis, it could signal an attack on aristocratic power.

Yet that power remained immense, and immensely resistant to the words (and actions) intermittently directed against it. Until the recent past, those in authority continued to believe, and to insist, that social order was inconceivable without the support of a visible hierarchy of birth. As the preceding chapter suggested, ideas about the state were for long coloured by the assumption that some men were born to command others. Machiavelli may have glimpsed a political community held together simply by the common citizenship of its members, but in this as in so much else his views were emphatically his own. The attitude of his younger contemporary Francesco Guicciardini was more characteristic of aristocratic opinion. Guicciardini came from a distinguished Florentine family; he wrote, as he explained, 'for the perpetual glory of his house'; and he seems to have taken for granted that political activity was a matter for those who were born to it. Intermittent popular revolt no doubt reinforced the conviction that respect for rank and birth was essential for the maintenance of civil order. The upheavals of seventeenth-century England drew to a close when Charles II won back his throne; and even before the King's return, control of local and parliamentary affairs was being restored – as Edward Hyde put it – 'to the government of the nobility and principal gentry'. After the turmoil of civil war and radical experiment, Hyde, like the rest of his class, took it for granted that the reimposition of order required the restoration both of crown and of aristocracy. The orderly community implied an orderly hierarchy of hereditary rank.

Rebellion against that hierarchy was in any case no light undertaking. The practical difficulties are obvious enough, but deserve mention. Only in early medieval times could the nobilities of Europe be described simply as a military elite; but over the centuries military leadership remained overwhelmingly an aristocratic vocation. The man on horseback – the knight, the *chevalier* – symbolized a noble's authority over those who went on foot; and he had the force to impose it on them. When peasant grievances spilled into violence, rebels frequently found themselves confronting landowners trained in arms. In the great rebellions which swept western France during the later 1630s, the noblemen of Périgord and Angoumois overcame their distaste for the government's financial demands and provided important support for royal forces in the reimposition of order. And as twentieth-century guerrillas have discovered, it was no easy matter to channel rural grievances into effective armed action. Poor communications hampered planning and organization beyond the level of the individual village; Engels long ago saw the intense parochialism of German country life as an important impediment to peasant militancy in 1525. Where armed action did succeed in getting under way, it was hard to sustain over time. The rhythms of a primitive economy imposed their own constraints, and erstwhile rebels often melted away at harvest time. In these circumstances, much clearly depended on the availability of able and inspiring leadership: leadership of the kind which Michael Gaismair provided for a time in the Tirolean revolts of the 1520s. But leaders came and went, more or less violently. Nothing is more suggestive of the fragility of mass movements in these conditions than the disintegration of the Peasants' Revolt in England after Wat Tyler's death at Smithfield in June 1381.

Here, it becomes hard to distinguish the practical from the psychological limitations on revolt. More often than not, peasant grievances attacked seigneurial abuses without calling into question the principle of aristocratic authority itself. The most celebrated résumés of the German countrymen in 1525 – those drafted at Hemmingen or later at Stuhlingen, for example – criticized financial 'innovations' by landowners, but proclaimed their loyalty to lordship as it had traditionally functioned. In 1594 peasant rebels in south-west France circulated a defence of their actions (which had included extensive violence against seigneurial property). This text catalogued the misdeeds of some members of the provincial nobility, and called on all 'gentlemen without reproach' to protect the community – the traditional function of the second estate – from their less scrupulous colleagues. As in the German documents, the manifesto included a declaration of support for the nobility as a whole.

Some historians have seen such evidence as a sign of the 'deference' which supposedly coloured the attitude of lesser men to their social betters. The idea has its uses, but it hardly does full justice to a complex relationship. There was nothing deferential about full-scale peasant rebellion, and the distinction between 'good' and 'bad' nobles, hinted at in the French manifesto of 1594, carried its own overtones of menace. Even when relations between lords and tenants were less fraught, 'deference' too easily suggests an unthinking acquiescence in aristocratic authority. In reality, peasant attitudes must often have involved a degree of shrewd calculation. The power of a nobleman was not necessarily to be seen as a negative or hostile force. It could, as we have seen, be turned to account: by providing advancement for individuals, or protecting the community from dangerous outsiders, whether invaders or tax-collectors. Disputes seem frequently to have involved bargaining rather than open violence. (Indeed some 'rebellions' probably stemmed from demonstrations or mass-meetings which got out of hand.) Well before the year 1000, we have already glimpsed country people from northern Italy in legal haggling over 'customary' payments to their lords. During the later fourteenth and early fifteenth centuries, a group of Midland tenants of the Earls of Warwick used a highly successful campaign of strikes and litigation to keep their rents low: and this in defiance of two of the most powerful noble families — the Beauchamps and Nevilles — in later medieval England. The attitude of such people towards aristocratic authority was no more characterized by unthinking deference than by systematic hostility. But it was precisely the systematic challenge to hereditary power that seems to have been so hard to formulate. In moments of exceptional turmoil, rebels occasionally glimpsed a possibility of radical change, cast most often in the language of religion. More frequently, their grievances echoed the character of aristocratic authority itself: in the demand for a return to customary relations between lord and tenant, or for the proper discharge of the lord's duties of protection and defence. When a Staffordshire man was gaoled for organizing mass poaching on the estates of the Earl of Uxbridge in 1763, his reaction was to petition the Earl for clemency, and appeal to the 'generosity and compassion' of the great man. This was no doubt a piece of calculated flattery. But generosity was the mark of the well-born, and even a man who had suffered at the hands of an aristocrat looked naturally to him for help. Popular acquiescence in aristocratic authority was neither constant nor uncritical. But even the rural poor rarely broke with the traditional association between hereditary rank and leadership in the community at large. When the French peasantry rose against aristocratic power in the *Jacquerie* of 1358, they blamed the nobility — their natural leaders — for recent military disasters in the English wars. Over the centuries, aristocracy was most vulnerable to popular criticism when gentlemen failed in their exercise of the authority to which they were born. And to this extent, the ruled shared the aristocratic assumptions of their rulers.

In the modern world, assumptions are very different. Men in power are unlikely to justify their position by an appeal to hereditary right, and the public would be unlikely to think much of the claim if they did so. The character of leadership has been transformed, and it will be the purpose of the remainder of this chapter to suggest some ways in which the transformation has come about.

Elites, old and new

Here it will be useful to dwell for a moment on one particular feature of aristocratic authority as it was traditionally exercised: that is its general or all-round character. Men born to exercise leadership could expect to do so in every important sphere of public life. This is not to say that noblemen at all times in the past enjoyed a monopoly of political power or material wealth. Success in business or government service regularly took new-comers into the ranks of the privileged. But once there, families of high status could expect to enjoy, and to pass on to later generations, a distinction which transcended mere specialist skills. The 'prudence' which moralists down the centuries so ceaselessly recommended was the essential trait of a governing class: a capacity to reflect and act on weighty problems, wherever they arose. Burke thought that it was the advantage of birth, and of an upbringing 'in a place of estimation', which enabled gentlemen to assume a wide-ranging leadership over the whole range of public affairs. This was not to defend a closed caste: talented recruits from business of the professions were essential if Burke's 'natural aristocracy' was to maintain its governing position. But 'talent' had to be rightly understood. The leaders of the community needed a capacity for 'the large view': not, or not only, a record of professional success. This was the reasoning behind Burke's famous tirades against the members of the French National Assembly in the early days of the Revolution. A great nation, so he claimed, had been hijacked by a gang of mere small-town lawyers wholly lacking in the inherited capacity for judgement, the broader political vision, which leadership in public life demanded. The ferocity of Burke's language was distinctively his own, but the nub of his argument was a familiar, and thoroughly aristocratic, one. Even rebellious country people found it hard to break free from the assumption that birth and rank conferred a general pre-eminence in the life of the community. Specialist skills carried no such weight. Opponents of army reform in Victorian England defended the purchase of commissions on precisely these grounds. Gentlemen of indepen-dent means wielded an authority which no mere professional could match; and, so it was claimed, their assured status made them less likely to go warmongering in pursuit of advancement. Six centuries earlier Thomas Aquinas had put the same argument to rather different use. Senior positions in the church, he thought, were often better filled not by a saint (another version of the professional specialist?) but by a man of rank and reputation. In the fullness of time, Thomas would himself become a saint; but he had been born a nobleman, and he no doubt appreciated the authority vested in the gentlemanly all-rounder. The cult of the amateur has its origins in the distinctive – because innate, hereditary, and hence general – character of aristocratic power.

Power in the modern world clearly operates in very different fashion. The claim that birth is a qualification for leadership is not generally heard (at least in public), and it is hard to associate any social group with the automatic pre-eminence in all fields that aristocracy once implied. In the complexities of an advanced industrial society, some political observers have denied the existence of any entrenched ruling elite, aristocratic or otherwise. This pluralist view of the problem has perhaps been taken furthest by Robert Dahl and his followers, who organized their analysis around the question: '*Who decides?*' They insisted that political clout cannot simply be inferred from a group's possession of great wealth or high status: power can be located only when the investigator demonstrates that in an identifiable conflict of interest, one party has prevailed over another. In Dahl's view Western democracies form a series of 'polyarchies', in which political factions, big businesses, trades unions and single-issue pressure groups jostle for power. This view of contemporary affairs could scarcely differ more drastically from the account of aristocracy suggested in this book. There is no place here for one group to exercise a general authority over the rest of the community: let alone an authority conceived as hereditary and innate.

The 'pluralist' analysis, it hardly needs adding, remains a controversial one. Dahl and his followers have usefully warned against assuming that a group's political weight forms a mere extension or expression of its wealth and status. But the argument has at times appeared to imply that social rank and economic resources are wholly irrelevant to the successful exercise of power; and this seems less than plausible. C. Wright Mills provided a rather different analysis of power in the modern world. Like Dahl, he emphasized the process of decision-making as a guide to the character of public life; unlike Dahl, he concluded that the process was leading to an ever-growing concentration of power. Where Dahl saw 'polyarchy', Mills saw 'the power elite'. Leadership in distinct, specialized fields – business, government, the armed services – was meshing into an irresistible and irresponsible unitary force. Here, unquestionably, were men who wielded power over the whole life of the community: who 'make news now, history later'.

But the aristocratic connotations of power have vanished almost as totally from this account of the modern elite as from Dahl's attempts to deny that the elite exists. High government officials, service chiefs, bank chairmen, appeared to Mills to be moving towards an even closer, and more sinister, fusion of interests. But their power was dependent on that of the institution which employed them. Away from the boardroom of Chase Manhattan, or from his office in the Pentagon or State Department, even the most imposing member of Mills's elite found himself 'powerless, poor, uncelebrated'. Individuals took their chance in a world dominated by giant impersonal corporations, and they prospered or failed according to the criteria which the corporations imposed. The aristocratic assumptions of the past suggested both that birth entitled some men to wield authority over others: and that (because innate) their authority extended beyond any precise professional or functional limits. Each of these assumptions had now apparently gone for good.

Some doubts remain. Analyses of this kind may explain away rather too much. The student of aristocratic power is not likely to underestimate the force of heredity in human affairs, the impulse to pass on a family's resources to the generations of the future. And he should have acquired some feel for the informal, elusive character of aristocratic power: the connection or 'pull' which men of influence exercised as they pursued their objectives within and beyond the formal institutions of government. It would be unreasonable to suppose that, in the century of the common man, these forces have wholly vanished. Modern vocabulary makes the point clearly enough. Behind the institutional facade of government department and financial corporation, private influence advances private (and family) fortunes: *enchufe* and *pistonnage* in the Hispanic and Francophone worlds, *blat* and *sottogoverno* in

Moscow and Rome. In the West, the private fortunes of Kennedys and Rockefellers have provided a springboard to political leadership. In the East, hereditary wealth has been abolished; but members of the *Nomenklatura* − those who control the means of administration in state and party − pass on to their children the fruits of educational and environmental advantage. For as long as the family survives, we can suppose that power will carry some association with heredity. But here *is* a decisive break with the aristocratic past. Once − as we have abundantly seen − birth was celebrated as a qualification for leadership, and a stimulus towards its worthy exercise. Now, the continuing advantages which birth confers provoke unease, dissimulation, or open hostility. Leadership is to be articulated in terms of competence or patriotism or ideological purity, however much those who exercise it may in practice owe to inherited wealth or private influence. It would be a strange (though not perhaps inconceivable) development if ambitious Americans or Russians were in future to base their claims to advancement on long-standing family connections in Congress or the Politburo: stranger still if their claims won widespread support. Such possibilities can be left to the expert observers of American or Soviet affairs. But to all appearances, the aristocratic character of power − the presumed link between authority and birth − has gone. In the modern world, leadership is proclaimed, and accepted, in other terms. And it is for the historian of aristocracy to explain in rather more detail how this change in the character of power has come about.

The challenge of modernity?

In 1790 Burke believed that the whole aristocratic order was under threat from the revolutionaries of France. But he thought that he glimpsed, behind the upheavals in Paris, the influence of other men: the radical intellectuals of the enlightenment. Helvetius, Rousseau, Voltaire, all appeared to Burke the indirect agents of the current anarchy: authors of an unprecedented attack on the claims of hierarchy and tradition. Over the preceding century or so, attitudes to hereditary rank had indeed undergone a good deal of change. Far more systematically than in the past, governments and their agents sought to eradicate the more disagreeable aspects of aristocratic authority. From Struensee in Denmark to Jovellanos in Spain, reforming ministers worked to reduce or abolish such 'feudal' survivals as the enforcement of labour services or the imposition of arbitrary seigneurial dues. When Charles-Emmanuel of Savoy introduced a series of land reforms in 1771, a popular song rejoiced that the rule of aristocracy was over and that the King's subjects would henceforth live as free men under the rule of their 'sovereign inspired by the goddess Humanity'. Even in Naples — hardly a hotbed of iconoclasm — things were stirring. Antonio Genovesi, professor of political economy from 1750, gave lectures on the evils of what he called feudalism: and a series of reform-minded ministers worked on plans for eroding the 'sacrosanct magnate-ism' which one of them described as dominating Neapolitan society.

As we saw in the preceding chapter, relations between state and aristocratic authority had never been wholly free of incident. But these eighteenth-century episodes contained some significant new ingredients. On an unprecedented scale, spokesmen for enlightened state power — 'cameralists' in the German-speaking lands — invoked the principles of humanity and utility to counter aristocratic traditions which they regarded as offensive. Around the middle of the eighteenth century, the point was vigorously made by an official who worked on law-reform in the electorate of Hanover: a thousand years of injustice, he said, were no basis for even a moment of legitimacy. In this, Burke was certainly right. The ideology of the enlightenment coexisted uneasily, if at all, with the claims of customs or long usage. A similar, Burkeian, note was sounded in 1807, by aristocratic critics of the Prussian decress which abolished serfdom; in the pursuit of equality before the law, they claimed, 'enlightened' legislators were destroying the patriarchal bonds between the greater and lesser men which had traditionally held the community together. A good deal of eighteenth-century thinking was certainly casual in its treatment of claims to hereditary rank. As late as 1678, a Frenchman named La Roque produced a treatise on nobility; and, in it, like so many before him, he mused on the mysterious process ('je ne sais quelle force') by which gentlemen passed on aristocratic distinction to their sons. La Roque's book was reprinted in the early eighteenth century, but by now sounded distinctly old-fashioned. Advanced thinkers had little time for the mysteries of blood or semen. In an increasingly secular intellectual environment, it was becoming harder to argue that God had ordered humanity in an immutable hierarchy of birth and rank. Readers of Montesquieu's *Spirit of the Laws* were more likely to reflect on the variety of social organization as communities adjusted to changing needs and resources. The original Greek sense of aristocracy had, after all, meant one form of constitution among others. More decisively than at any stage in the intervening centuries, the thinkers of the Enlightenment returned to the idea. The nobilities of Europe, with their elaborate gradations of rank and privilege, were the products of history, of human experience over time: not the expression of a divine plan, nor of a universal natural order.

The change was, at least potentially, a momentous one. This secularized understanding of history, and of social hierarchy, had been fleetingly expressed on numerous occasions before the eighteenth century. But it was then that it gained wide currency for the first time. Its implications were dramatic. If the present ordering of society was simply the product of the needs and experiences of the past, there was no obvious argument against social reorganization as needs changed. Aristocratic power might once have been of service to the community: Montesquieu pointed out that the apparent barbarities of medieval law-codes had their own rationale in the conditions of the time. But conditions changed, and now it was becoming possible to envisage a future in which the utility of aristocratic power was exhausted. The break with traditional attitudes could hardly have been more striking. Change need no longer be justified by appeals to a more or less idealized past. Order in the community need no longer be conceived as dependent on the innate authority which some men wielded over others. All subsequent radicalism started from the propostion that social hierarchy was a historical construction: and hence capable of being reconstructed − or flattened.

But there was an obvious irony in all this. A link can undoubtedly be traced between the social theories of the Enlightenment and the overtly revolutionary ideologies of more recent times. Yet Montesquieu and the rest would have been astonished to find themselves cast as script-writers for Saint Just or Paine or the young Marx. Many of them (like Montesquieu) were, after all, themselves noblemen. So were many of their readers; and so were the reform-minded government ministers who attacked disagreeable aristocratic behaviour in the name of 'humanity' and 'utility'. This was the point. None of these men had the slightest intention of undermining the position of the established ruling class. But the nobility must demonstrate its usefulness to the community; appeals to tradition or a divinely-ordered hierarchy were no longer intellectually respectable. Neither were the old aristocratic taboos on the too-zealous pursuit of wealth. Noblemen must accommodate themselves more easily to those who had made fortunes in the City or overseas. This was Condorcet's point when he insisted on the need for equality in political life: equal rights for all substantial owners of property whatever its form, and no rights for those who owned none. The claims of wealth or talent or utility advanced, those of blood or tradition receded. But the nobility remained unquestionably the governing class. The Prussian legislation of 1807 invoked good Enlightened principles to justify the abolition of serfdom: henceforth each individual could seek advancement to the limits of his ability. Despite conservative warnings, aristocratic landowners continued to dominate Prussian public life nevertheless.

In the very long run, it may be that the conservatives were right. Eighteenth-century theorists placed aristocracy squarely in the context of man-made social institutions, and so exposed it to the possibility of criticism in quite unprecedented terms. In 1799 Madame de Stael glimpsed some of the issues which were at stake. She noted in horror that revolutionary extremists were advocating the abolition of property: they even dared to claim that this followed logically from the principles of the Enlightenment. De Stael and those like her inevitably found the radical line of argument absurd as well as alarming. Eighteenth-century criticism – 'the reasoning which has overturned slavery, and feudalism, and heredity', as de Stael approvingly put it – was designed to rationalize the power of the propertied elite, not to undermine it. In the uneasy aftermath of the Revolution, de Stael was already able to sense where these principles might lead. But in their eighteenth-century context, the principles had appeared altogether less subversive: an adjustment of aristocratic culture to changing social and intellectual conditions.

In more recent times, the problem of adjustment has become more acute. Social commentators over the centuries had discussed the mishaps or extinction of great aristocratic families. The disappearance of ancient names, like the emergence of new ones, testified to the mysterious workings of providence, or to the capricious play of fortune's wheel. But by the nineteenth century the theme was changing. By now it was possible to discuss failure in terms not of individual (or family) misfortune, but of the erosion of aristocratic authority as a whole. In the memoirs which he published in 1848, Chateaubriand applied his incomparable, if melancholy, prose to a chronicle of gradual aristocratic decline: from power, through privilege, to mere contemporary vanity. Two decades on, Bagehot's celebrated account of the English constitution placed the hereditary peerage firmly among the 'dignified' components of the system. Like the monarch herself, the House of Lords represented political window-dressing: real power – what Bagehot called 'efficient' power – lay elsewhere. His point was indirectly borne out by the Liberal crisis of 1886. In that year, the bulk of the Whig grandees abandoned the Liberal party for Conservatism, and aristocracy became in effect associated with specifically Tory sympathies. A hereditary elite, the natural leadership in all political groupings, was turning into one party (or a part of one party) among others. Birth had traditionally conferred authority over the whole range of public affairs: now, apparently, no longer. What lay behind the change?

One obvious factor was economic and social development. Railways would break the traditional tyranny of rank and deference: the thought occurred to Dr Arnold as he watched a locomotive draw out of Rugby station, and the observation became a commonplace among social commentators throughout mid-nineteenth-century Europe. We can turn the remark into a more general point: that there are certain forms of rapid material change with which aristocratic power – for all its adaptability – has found it hard to cope.

As we have seen, aristocratic attitudes towards wealth had always been complex, with deep-rooted prejudices for and against particular forms both of getting and of spending. But wealth was nevertheless essential. Nobilities needed the resources to display and finance their leadership in the community as a whole. The immensely increased pace of economic change – represented above all by colonial expansion and the early stages of industrialization – meant a wholly unprecedented shift in the balance between aristocratic and non-aristocratic fortunes. This was the

point made by a writer for *The Economist* in 1864. Unlike
Bagehot, he thought that public life in England remained
essentially aristocratic, and that birth still counted for much: but
to the really rich man — 'with £10,000 a year clear' — all doors
were open, whatever his origins and whatever the sources of his
wealth. Rich newcomers were as old as aristocracy itself, as we
have repeatedly seen. But now fortunes were to be made more
rapidly, in greater numbers, and in a wider range of activities,
than ever before; and perhaps most important, not all those who
applied their wealth to a political career hoped to turn gentleman
in the process. In the age of the first millionaire radicals — Joseph
Chamberlain was starting his career in Birmingham politics
during the 1860s — the old association between high rank and
public leadership was losing a good deal of its force. Wealth
corroded those traditional links in other ways as well. When
Hugh Grosvenor was created Duke of Westminster in 1874, his
qualification for the title was straightforward: he was colossally
rich. The immense revenues of their properties in Belgravia and
Mayfair took the Grosvenors to the highest rank in the English
peerage, customarily associated with members (legitimate and
otherwise) of the royal family and with national heroes like
Marlborough or Wellington. The forebears of the first Duke of
Westminster bequeathed him no tradition of leadership or
distinction in public life: nor have his successors established one.
Great wealth had always provided a route towards the power and
distinction of aristocratic leadership. But now there were signs
that the role of wealth was changing. Some rich men ignored or
rejected hereditary distinction as they made their way in the
political world; others combined high rank with total indifference
to any public function. Power and rank, to put it crudely, were
available on the open market: and each could be purchased
independently of the other. Centuries of aristocratic tradition
assumed that gentlemen were natural leaders in the life of the
community. In the England of Bagehot or Chamberlain, or the
first Duke of Westminster, that venerable principle seemed to be
losing something of its force.

Dignified retreat

We might conclude from this that economics was decisive in

eroding aristocratic power, or in reducing the aristocratic interest to one pressure group among others. Many nineteenth-century observers certainly did so, as they linked the revolutions in transport technology and industrial organization to the end of deference and privilege. And there are no doubt some extremely general correlations to be observed between the economic structure of a community and the power of an aristocracy to maintain a hold over it. In the agrarian economy of the Middle Ages, aristocratic power was rooted in control of the land. When the economic significance of land was eventually swamped by the commercial and industrial sectors, artistocratic influence faced corresponding problems of adjustment. Essentially, these generalizations concern the material resources available to nobles and to other influential groups within the community: the shifting relative proportions of aristocratic and non-aristocratic wealth. It is of obvious importance to establish when, and in what circumstances, a nobility has found itself financially out-gunned by industrialists or financiers. A shifting economic balance implied new limits to aristocratic power. But crude determinism is to be avoided. The history of aristocracy in recent times cannot be reduced to an essay on 'the corroding power of money', important though that unquestionably was. Aristocratic authority had always involved more than the economic resources which fuelled it. Rulers and ruled shared a view of hierarchy and the claims of birth from which it proved, even in moments of social upheaval, hard to escape. In the transformed landscape of the industrial nineteenth century, these inherited assumptions retained much of their influence: even (perhaps especially) in England, the most advanced economy of them all. Aristocratic culture had a momentum, or at least a staying-power, of its own.

The influence of noblemen over the rest of the community has certainly proved tenacious. Down to the First World War, the crack regiments in most European armies retained a strongly aristocratic tone; when a detachment of the Household Cavalry reached Egypt in 1882, every officer was a peer, or a peer's son. Much the same was true of the more prestigious government departments. In Bismark's Germany, young noblemen joined smart student fraternities at Jena or Königsberg and went on to work alongside their university *Korpsbrudern* in the finance ministry or the diplomatic service. Aristocratic influence had deep local influence and deep local roots as well. The park and the big house provided visible reminders of hereditary distinction, and the squire, or *Monsieur le Vicomte*, was widely thought an appropriate chairman for charitable societies or the local association for agricultural improvement. As late as the 1950s, voters in the conservative western departments of France showed a marked inclination to elect noblemen as mayors. The 'aristocratic particle' − as in *de* Gaulle or *d'*Estaing − is a notoriously unreliable guide to actual ancestry, and its use in contemporary France has provided a regular subject for controversy or derision. But bogus or not, the signs of aristocratic distinction have only very slowly lost their power over the rest of the community.

Nowhere has this been more true than in England. As we have seen, unprecedented economic change suggested to many Victorian observers that a decisive transfer of power was taking place: that leadership in public life was passing from those born to it, to those whose success in industry and commerce was transforming the very character of the community. Rule by gentlemen would give place to rule by manufacturers and entrepreneurs. But would it? Bonaparte had called the English a nation of shopkeepers; yet the shopkeepers proved remarkably respectful towards aristocratic authority. Despite a colossal expansion in urban wealth, and a gradual widening of the parlimentary franchise, the character of public life changed far less dramatically than conservatives had feared or radicals hoped. To the end of his career, Richard Cobden − that great spokesman for the manufacturing interest − deplored the tendency of English businessmen 'to prostrate themselves at the feet of feudalism' and abandon commerce for the life of a gentleman. As we saw at the beginning of chapter 3, a Yorkshire carpet-tycoon gravitated naturally towards a baronetcy and an estate in rural East Anglia; and that was in 1863, just two years before Cobden's death. These patterns of behaviour have cast a long shadow. For many Victorian entrepreneurs, the creation of wealth seems to have represented only a means towards social distinction and the possibility of political influence. And in nineteenth-century England, 'distinction' and 'influence' continued to carry marked aristocratic overtones. Such attitudes allowed little scope for the systematic pursuit of profit as an end in itself; and it has been argued with some plausibility that the competitive edge of the

British economy was permanently blunted as a result. In these circumstances, aristocratic influence was unlikely to find itself swept aside by a new ruling class of businessmen and industrialists. Not all Victoria's subjects shared the old assumption that public affairs were primarily a matter for gentlemen, but both then and later it retained considerable influence in English life. Commentators from the Continent or from the United States – Alexis de Tocqueville, or the Bostonian James Russell Lowell – noted that, more than elsewhere, power in mid-nineteenth-century England remained the concern of a hereditary ruling class. This was perhaps to be expected in a country where so much public authority had traditionally been vested in the hands of Lord-Lieutenants and Justices of the Peace. In a compact and homogeneous kingdom, English rulers down the centuries had been able to entrust the supervision of local affairs largely to the greater landowners of the shires. 'Aristocratic it was from the start': this was F. W. Maitland's epitaph on the old system when the newly established county councils replaced it in 1888. Far back into the medieval past, England had largely been run by well-born amateurs. By the later nineteenth century, the scale of government had become (in the most literal sense) imperial, but old attitudes lived on. In 1875 young Frederick Lugard – later one of the most distinguished African proconsuls – decided to sit the entrance examination for the Indian Civil Service: colonial administration, he reflected, was a 'thoroughly gentlemanly occupation'. At home or in the Empire, gentlemen ruled. Some inherited a claim to wield power. Others were channelled towards it through the fast-growing public schools, where a costly and idiosyncratic education turned boys from a variety of backgrounds into the 'natural' leaders of the community. In Victorian England, public authority retained a good deal of the aristocratic character discussed throughout this book: not least in the claim that one group of people enjoyed an innate right (hereditary or acquired) to give orders to the rest.

The end of aristocracy

But things were changing. Many of the foreign observers who remarked on the tenacity of aristocratic influence in Victorian

England thought it exceptional, at odds with the spirit of the age. Across the Atlantic, a great republic embodied the principle that a distinctive ruling class was superfluous – and probably harmful – to the government of a free people. In the aftermath of the American Revolution, ex-officers of the victorious army formed the Order of the Cincinnati: perhaps (as some contemporaries feared) in the attempt to create a hereditary aristocracy from scratch. But the episode was short lived. At the end of the nineteenth century, smart boarding schools on the east coast were claiming to groom their alumni for leadership on the English model; yet the products of Groton or St Paul's gravitated far more readily towards business than into politics and public life. The style and education of a gentleman were easily enough exported: less so the assumption that gentlemanly rank conferred authority over others. Even in England, that assumption was proving increasingly controversial. Aristocratic power fought a remark-ably successful rearguard action – far more successful than critics like Cobden or Joseph Chamberlain would have wished – but it was a rearguard action nevertheless. In his *Autobiography* (written in the 1870s, but published posthumously in 1883) Anthony Trollope insisted that some posts in public life were of such importance that they could scarcely be filled except by 'gentle-men'. Remarks of this kind had been commonplace down the centuries; and, as we have seen, many of Trollope's contempor-aries continued to think along these distinctly aristocratic lines. Many, but not all; as Trollope was well aware. An old cliché of social observation, shared by nobles and non-nobles alike, was becoming a matter for contention and debate. The claims of birth and rank were going out of fashion, Trollope thought, and best not proclaimed in public – whatever friends might murmur among themselves.

There may have been an element of literary affectation in Trollope's diagnosis, but its general drift was accurate enough. Once the community had broadly endorsed the innate authority of the well-born; now opinion was increasingly divided. The whole character of public life was changing, and in the process acquiescence in aristocratic leadership was wearing away. In the same year that Trollope published his *Autobiography*, an English Cabinet minister (Joseph Chamberlain) startled the country with his outspoken attacks on aristocratic power – 'the insolent pretensions of an hereditary caste'. Political leadership was to be a task for the public-spirited and the successful — like Chamberlain — not a birthright of the privileged. Over much of nineteenth-century Europe, attacks on rank and hierarchy became as widespread as their acceptance had once been. The phenomenon is hard to describe, let alone to explain, without drifting into a résumé of the whole course of recent history. Economic change undoubtedly played a part. Industrialization — a process mainly beyond noble control — tipped the balance of wealth away from aristocratic fortunes. Unprecedented urban growth meant that huge populations were living and working in a setting where traditional patterns of aristocratic influence were hard to maintain. The secular ideologies of the nineteeth century confronted aristocratic authority more directly still. Rebels in the past had found it as hard to formulate systematic criticism of the social hierarchy as to organize and sustain effective resistance to the power of noblemen. Now social theorists planned confidently for a future without aristocracy. In a striking break with tradition, Tom Paine's *Rights of Man* praised Wat Tyler and the English rebels of 1381 as better men, and greater public benefactors, than the barons who had faced King John at Runnymede. The nationalist fervour which swept so much of the Continent during the nineteenth century took little account of the distinctive claims of birth and rank. And the various prophets of socialism — heirs to the most subversive implications of the Enlightenment — explicitly denied them. For all its persistent influence, aristocracy seemed set on a collision course with the most powerful currents of modern opinion.

In the light of all this, some contemporary aristocrats have weathered the storms with marked success. Where governments have not abolished it, private wealth has proved extremely durable: not least when it has been transmitted down the generations in the aristocratic form of great houses and art collections and grouse moors. Nobles survive and prosper as bankers, connoisseurs, socialites, breeders of racehorses or owners of safari parks. Wealth and style have a force of their own, and we should be unwise to discount the play of discreet aristocratic influence in the contemporary world. But 'discreet' is crucial. Once, the connection between rank and power, between birth and a claim to authority, had been openly proclaimed and broadly accepted. Down the centuries, leadership in the community had been a matter for those with a distinctive right to exercise it; and the exercise of power in turn reinforced men's claim to membership of a distinctive, and largely hereditary, elite. This is no longer so. Power has lost its aristocratic associations.

In part, this reflects the barrage of criticism directed by radical opponents against the hereditary principle of public life. Hierarchy, and the distinctive claims of birth, have come to seem irrational and outmoded bases for the ordering of the community: and not only radicals have come to think them so. Even those who inherited rank and title gradually learned to see themselves as citizens among other citizens, albeit particularly rich or well-regarded ones. When the French National Assembly abolished feudal dues and aristocratic privileges on the night of 4 August 1789, many noblemen supported the decision. The Marquis de Ferrières − not a radical − thought that the unity of the nation was now greater than in twelve centuries of traditional, hierarchical government. Anachronistic privilege had gone; rich and poor stood together as citizens of France. And already, in 1789, this was an outcome which many nobles were eager to applaud.

The retreat of privilege has, of course, turned out to be a slow and ambiguous process. Until a very recent past, it was easily assumed that full political rights were for property-owners (or for adult males) only. Enormous disparities of wealth have frequently made nonsense of formal equality before law or constitution. And if the aristocratic link between birth and authority is no longer taken seriously, this is in part because the nineteenth and twentieth centuries have provided numerous more plausible justifications for massive inequalities of wealth or power. In this, Shakespeare's Ulysses has been proved wrong. 'Degree' − that natural hierarchy which set noblemen above their inferiors − has indeed vanished, as Ulysses warned that it might. But the predicted anarchy − 'and hark what discord follows' − has not materialized. Nor has equality. Heredity and rank have ceased to provide a cement for the social order, but, in the hands of financiers or apparatchiks, concentrations of wealth and power remain: justified in the name of the free market, or of the party and the revolution. In the contemporary world, elites flourish, whatever precise sense we attach to that term for winners in the pursuit of leadership and prestige. Yet the rules of the game have, slowly, been redrawn. In public life, the language of citizenship had gradually replaced that of birth and honour. This has not entailed the inevitable disappearance of aristocrats from all positions of influence. 'Everything must change in order that everything can remain the same,' declared a character in di Lampedusa's novel *The Leopard*; even in the upheavals of the mid-nineteenth century, Sicilian noblemen might continue to run the island's political life. But they had to stake a new claim to leadership: commitment to the cause of national independence, not the innate authority conferred by blood and name.

So some aristocrats survived. Given the financial resources which many inherited, it is hardly surprising that they should have done so. A number adapted to the demands of mass politics and achieved success or notoriety in a transformed public life. The career of a Churchill, or a Mosley, may hint at lingering aristocratic advantages, at least in Britain earlier this century. A duke's cousin or a sixth baronet moved perhaps more freely between political allegiances than those whose rise from obscurity bound them more closely to the party cause. Nevertheless men and women in power no longer claim it as their birthright. Leadership is exercised, and made legitimate, in other terms: in terms of commitment to programmes and competence in pursuing them. Aristocrats are not an extinct species. But in its oldest and most potent sense — the innate authority which set one group of people over the rest — aristocracy has gone.

Some Remarks on Further Reading

Any kind of systematic bibliography would fill many volumes larger than the present one. The following comments offer no more than some highly subjective pointers towards significant contributions to the subject. First, a number of case-studies: analyses of aristocratic power as it operated in specific places at specific times.

An immense body of scholarship centres on the emergence of the medieval nobility. By the eleventh century a number of features were appearing which did much to shape the later character of aristocracy: the preoccupation with hereditary descent, the feudal language of land-use and military obligation, the cult of knighthood. Were these developments new? How much did they inherit from an ill-documented past, even from Roman times? This is difficult territory, and some of its most important features have long been clouded by controversy. Nevertheless, guides exist. The French historian Georges Duby − a prolific and imaginative author − provides a number of starting-points: recently, for example, in *The Chivalrous Society* (1977). In *The Medieval Nobility* (1979) T. Reuter edited and translated a sample of current continental work. Marc Bloch's *Feudal Society* was completed in 1940 and expertise in the field has inevitably overtaken a good deal of its content since then. But it remains a remarkably vivid and attractive attempt to depict a whole historical landscape. And Bloch's analysis of lordship − aristocratic authority over lesser men − is especially germane to the concerns of the present book.

For later periods, recent scholarship has provided powerful evidence for the durability and adaptability of aristocratic power. The work of K. B. McFarlane offers a case in point. The intermittent disorders of the later Middle Ages had long been associated with aristocratic decadence: the Wars of the Roses, a by-word for atavistic baronial thuggery. In *The Nobility of Later Medieval England* (published posthumously in 1973) McFarlane presented a very different picture. Here, and in a number of less accessible papers and essays, the nobility appeared as the natural leaders of the community with an equally natural interest in staving off civil disorder, not in promoting it. Nobles were expected to wield authority, and − the occasional wastrel or psychopath apart − most had the training, the financial resources and the political sense to be able to do so. A rather similar picture emerges from the collected essays of J. H. Hexter, published in 1961 as *Reappraisals in History*. The period of Renaissance and Reformation brought obvious intellectual and social change, but, in the main, nobles managed to adapt; and Hexter argued with characteristic elegance that their successful adaptation was an essential starting-point for an understanding of the times. Even the growth of the great territorial states has come to appear less destructive of aristocratic power than was once believed. Chapter 4 of this book has suggested some reasons why this should be so. In *Lineages of the Absolutist State* (1974), Perry Anderson builds a case on very different ideological foundations; but the completed construction is a powerful account of the interests which bound governments and noblemen together.

There are some helpful accounts of aristocracy's slow retreat. General surveys include G. Chaussinand-Nogaret, *Histoire des Elites 1700–1848* and D. Spring (ed.), *European Landed Elites in the Nineteenth Century*, published in 1975 and 1977 respectively. In the context of one nation's experience, F. M. L. Thompson's *English Landed Society in the Nineteenth Century* (1963) traces the course of aristocratic adjustment to industrialization and democracy. Power gave way to influence, and aristocracy became one elite among others: no longer that unique concentration of authority and rank to which all ambitious newcomers had once aspired. Thompson emphasized the tenacity with which aristocratic influence lingered on, down to the bloody caesura of the First World War. And the same point is abundantly illustrated in W. L. Guttsmann's *The English Ruling Class* (1960): a substantial and entertaining selection of nineteenth-century and early twentieth-century texts. The obsession with aristocratic and gentlemanly style has shaped the whole course of British social and economic development, and left the world's first industrial nation profoundly suspicious of profit and productivity: so argues Martin Wiener in *English Culture and the Decline of the Industrial Spirit* (1981). The case as put may raise further questions. Why, for example, should aristocratic values prove so much more resistant to 'the industrial spirit' in England than in Belgium or Germany? But whatever its substantive merits, Wiener's theme has an important bearing on the fortunes of aristocracy in the recent past. Power ebbed away; but a class which once controlled the education system, which once set the tone for fashion in the arts and social life, might exercise some posthumous hold over the behaviour and ideas of later generations.

Three contributions deserve special mention. In 1929–30, Lewis (later Sir Lewis) Namier published *The Structure of Politics at the Accession of George III*, and *England in the Age of the American Revolution*. Namier's work broke new ground both in content and in method. In unprecedented detail he examined the mechanics of aristocratic patronage; and he demonstrated the value of systematic biographical investigation – 'historical prosopography' is the discouraging technical term – both of the great men and of the smaller fry who inhabited the world of Hanoverian politics. Half a century on, Namier's studies are open to some obvious criticisms. Important though it is, patronage has never provided the whole basis of aristocratic power. In eighteenth-century England, as elsewhere, that power has also taken other, harsher, forms, such as the enactment of a ferocious penal code in defence of landed property. On this, and on the resources which financed aristocratic leadership, Namier had little to say. His work has also been judged too indifferent to the part played in public life by ideology or policy. This may reflect Namier's long immersion in historical sources of a particular kind – family papers and the records of day-to-day political manoeuvre – and his complex personality may also be a relevant issue. But whatever its limits, his work remains essential reading for the student of aristocracy: an unsurpassed analysis of a distinctive kind of power exercised by a distinctive class of people.

A decade later – published in the first week of the Second World War – Ronald Syme's *The Roman Revolution* made its appearance. Traditionally, accounts of the transition from Roman Republic to Roman Empire had been dominated by the commanding figure of Augustus. Syme directed his attention elsewhere: to the changing composition and fortunes of the senatorial aristocracy. In its minute dissection of party structures and individual careers, the approach may owe something to Namier. But Syme's manner was distinctively his own. He portrayed the potential brutality of aristocratic rule with particular force: both in relations between political rivals and in the treatment meted out to the lower orders. Slogans and ideologies – 'political catchwords' is Syme's characteristic phrase – received due attention. The result is a striking glimpse of aristocratic power and aristocratic attitudes as the community's natural leaders grappled with revolutionary upheaval two thousand years ago.

1965 saw the publication of perhaps the most ambitious case-study yet seen. In *The Crisis of the Aristocracy*, Lawrence Stone surveyed the economic, political and cultural activities of the greatest English families over the century which preceded the Civil War. Much in Stone's massive analysis remains controversial. Some experts have doubted whether landowners suffered economic difficulties as acute as Stone claimed. The English peerage – Stone's principal subject – may not provide a wholly satisfactory social category, since it excludes untitled younger sons. And the very notion of 'crisis' applies uneasily to a class which was to maintain its dominance over English life long after the seventeenth century. But the book is unique none the less: a monument of appropriately lavish scale.

Stone's intention – and his achievement – was to construct an account of every important aspect of aristocratic life: from estate-management, to court intrigue, to the funeral ceremonies which marked the departure of a great man. The attempt to provide a complete picture of a given historical environment meant more than a massive addition to the stock of scholarly knowledge. As Stone himself pointed out, it implied a conscious choice of historical method, and in particular a readiness to import into the study of the past insights and techniques derived from other disciplines.

Throughout much of the present century, historians have urged one another to look to, and to draw on, the achievements of social scientists or psychologists or students of linguistics. Interdisciplinary exchanges have a good deal to offer the student of aristocracy. The work of political scientists on elites in the modern world provides one standard by which to assess the very different character of aristocratic rule in the past. T. B. Bottomore's *Elite and Society* and Geraint Parry's *Political Elites* – first published in 1964 and 1969 respectively – offer convenient approaches to the issue and in particular to the work, discussed in the main text, of such theorists as Dahl and Wright Mills. Anthropologists have often proved more sensitive than historians to the connections between power and display; and this has obvious bearing on the aristocratic passion for making rank visible. The ceremonies of life at Versailles, for example, are easily written of as empty ostentation. In *The Court Society* – only recently (1983) available in English – Norbert Elias has argued that on the contrary etiquette embodied a highly political meaning: a balancing act between king and potentially troublesome noble clienteles. Anthropologists have also devoted considerable attention to the ways in which order can be maintained in the absence of formal governmental institutions. Max Gluckman's celebrated papers on feud and rebellion in tribal Africa gave wide currency to the theme from the 1950s onwards. Here, too, light may be thrown on the aristocratic past. Systems of blood feud and compensation were perhaps less anarchic than historians had traditionally supposed; they might offer a means for great men to arrange arbitration and peace-making among their kinspeople and followers. In *The Long-Haired Kings* (1962), J. M. Wallace-Hadrill's essay on feud provided a stimulating application of this argument to the conditions of early medieval Europe. Order is not synonymous with the existence of formal governing institutions, nor unattainable in their absence. This suggests a good deal about the resolution of disputes, the containment of violence and the exercise of aristocratic leadership in earlier centuries. But historians are likely to move on to other questions. In what circumstances, following what changes in material or cultural conditions, have 'informal systems of control' come to appear inadequate? Why was elaborate government machinery increasingly seen as necessary for the maintenance of order? The social scientists rightly encourage the historian to identify the meaning or function of a phenomenon: to locate the role of feud, for example, within a larger system of power. But the historian also examines those systems over time. And time implies change – whether spectacular or barely perceptible – and the need to account for it. However fruitfully their paths may sometimes cross, students of different disciplines travel in pursuit of different objectives.

But it would be wrong to leave the last word on further reading to the academics, whatever their specialism. Aristocracy, after all, has left its own distinctive mark on the literature of the West. In every period the verse, drama, and novels of the time (the third-rate as much as the illustrious) have had much to say about the power and style of the well-born. *Beowulf's* heroes took up arms against the aliens and monsters of the early Germanic world. A generation ago, Evelyn Waugh — more tellingly in his novels of wartime than in the overexposed *Brideshead Revisited* — recorded the declining hold of birth and honour in an unsympathetic age. Over the intervening centuries, literature provides glimpses of aristocracy in all its forms: from Froissart's knights, through Castiglione's courtiers, to the parvenus and snobs who people the hunting stories of R. S. Surtees. Indeed 'reading' extends beyond books to all the survivals of aristocratic culture. Paintings and great houses and funeral monuments can be 'read', as statements by and about the families which commissioned them. Aristocratic power has gone. But evidence of what its character once was is visible around us still.

Index